≫≪≫≪≫≪≫≪≫≪≫≪≫≪≫≪≫≪≫≪≫≪≫≪

Management and Leadership in Higher Education

Applying Modern Techniques of Planning, Resource Management, and Evaluation

Chester O. McCorkle, Jr.
Sandra Orr Archibald

Management and Leadership in Higher Education

Jossey-Bass Publishers

San Francisco • Washington • London • 1982

MANAGEMENT AND LEADERSHIP IN HIGHER EDUCATION
*Applying Modern Techniques of Planning, Resource Management,
and Evaluation*
by Chester O. McCorkle, Jr., and Sandra Orr Archibald

Copyright © 1982 by: Jossey-Bass Inc., Publishers
433 California Street
San Francisco, California 94104
&
Jossey-Bass Limited
28 Banner Street
London EC1Y 8QE

Library of Congress Cataloging in Publication Data

McCorkle, Chester O.
Management and leadership in higher education.

Bibliography: p. 221
Includes index.
1. Universities and colleges—Administration.
I. Archibald, Sandra Orr. I. Title.
LB2341.M36   1982   378'.1   82-48073
ISBN 0-87589-532-8

Manufactured in the United States of America

The paper in this book meets the guidelines for
permanence and durability of the Committee on
Production Guidelines for Book Longevity of the
Council on Library Resources.

JACKET DESIGN BY WILLI BAUM

FIRST EDITION

Code 8225

*The Jossey-Bass
Series in Higher Education*

ᴥᴥᴥ Foreword

In this significant book, Chester McCorkle and Sandra Archibald demonstrate that the problems currently facing colleges and universities virtually demand increased attention to their management, and they go further by indicating just how colleges and universities can meet these problems through effective management practices.

It is, of course, not new for higher education institutions to face problems that require improved administration. Some readers will remember the Depression, when faculty members went for years without salary increases, campus facilities deteriorated, and colleges and universities, along with all institutions of society, suffered severe financial deprivation. Most readers will recall the demands that society made on higher education after World War II, when it substantially increased its pressure on institutions to increase research, to provide undergraduate education for unprecedented numbers of students, and to satisfy the need for new knowledge and advanced training in the academic disciplines and in the professions. Although gaps occasionally occurred between societal demands and needed resources, the administrative problems of the 1950s were not pri-

ix

marily financial. The needs were important; the status of universities was high; public and private commitment was substantial; and the funds were there. Determining an intelligent rate of growth, maintaining quality in the process, and intelligently applying the ever-increasing resources—these were the main management tasks of institutional leaders.

In the 1960s, the campuses became the principal sites at which substantial social, political, and cultural issues were confronted: the civil rights movement, the controversy about the war in Vietnam, concern with the environment, and the systematic challenge to the value and authority of established institutions. No one was prepared to cope with the new styles of protest employed in these movements, and universities were uniquely vulnerable to them. At the time, the pervasiveness and strength of these trends were dimly understood, enormously frightening to the society as a whole, and seemingly more a consequence of indulgence, ineptitude, and gullibility on the part of colleges and universities than a manifestation of major changes in society at large. During this period, the overriding task of university leaders was to maintain the integrity of the institution, to keep it from becoming a captured instrument of political action, to retain its commitment to rationality and civility. Because of the widespread distaste for what was occurring on the campuses, the task of administrators in increasing public understanding of those events and in maintaining public support was enormous.

These periods were not, of course, as distinctively different as this brief description would suggest; one set of problems slid almost imperceptibly into the next. They did, however, give rise to different management problems and call for different management skills. None of them, however, required attention to the range of management theory and skill with as much urgency as will the next several decades. The problems looming ahead make this book especially timely.

Higher education has remained high in the national priority, but since the 1960s it has gained many competitors for both the public and the private dollar—among them, health, welfare, the environment. Competition with these other worthy causes for funds is intense, and the resources available for all of them are shrinking. Demographic and economic factors are challenging enrollment assumptions. Support from the federal government for research funds is clearly decreasing. Scholarships and fellowships for graduate and professional training are destined to decline. Institutional student aid funds will be under increasing pressure. The changing nature of employment requirements has markedly altered student interests and hence curriculum planning and patterns.

It is obviously no longer possible, if indeed it ever was, for the university to be all things to all men and women—to meet all demands with equal strength. The need is now growing to set priorities, to choose to expand in one area and contract in another, to distinguish functions that are necessary from those that are merely desirable. This required reallocation of resources —reducing or dropping something established while beginning something new—will place the decision-making process of the university under enormous strain. In the past, for the most part, accommodating new needs involved at most a fair, sensible, and intelligent queuing of university units in the order in which they would receive the new funds, new buildings, or additional staff. Rarely did the situation require the diversion of resources, space, money, or personnel from one area to another. This queuing process was not without anguish, but the pain was not as intense as it is becoming under the new conditions. Since very little of what a university does is frivolous or worthless, the choices are difficult. (In my experience, the least defensible activities also produce the least amount of money to be reallocated.) No defensible activity lacks a constituency capable of vigorous defense of its function, both inside and outside the university, and end-runs to trustees, professional associations, mass media, and the public are completely predictable.

All of this makes it mandatory that the decision-making process be visible and fair, with ample opportunity for each case to be made carefully and fully with special attention to ensure that the procedure is as free as possible from politics and special privilege. It requires the rational, self-conscious, open, and deliberate process of institutional management that this book describes.

In the following chapters, Chester McCorkle and Sandra Archibald make clear that the basic management functions of planning, resource allocation, and evaluation involve all segments of the institutional community. Even though the intelligent application and sensitive adaptation of these procedures is ultimately the responsibility of administrators, all segments of the community have equally important obligations to respect and use these processes with equal integrity. A college or university has no divine right to exist and must serve the society that supports it; this is equally true of an institution's constituent parts. Individual units have no constitutional mandate for their continued existence or for a perpetual claim on resources.

If the institution is to survive under constricting conditions, some long-standing habits will have to change—habits of competitiveness and special pleading and derogation of other competitors. There must be a renewed sensitivity to the needs of the university itself, a dedication to its welfare, and a willingness to subordinate one's own desires and those of one's group to the common interest. Unfortunately, these are not pronounced tendencies among us, and the years of relative affluence I referred to earlier did not strengthen them. Members of the university community have grown to regard the university as an instrumentality for satisfying their own needs and aspirations, with little thought to corresponding responsibilities to the institution itself. It is my solemn message that this posture will have to change markedly.

The university consists of interdependent parts, and the welfare of each is closely tied to the strength of the institution as a whole. I am reminded of the conception of the common good held by the founders of this republic. The public good was not, as it is viewed today, the sum or average of the interests of community segments weighted by their political power. Rather, the ideal governance process was one in which these particular interests were transcended through the recognition and attainment of larger, common goals. For this reason, the founders emphasized the importance of what they called public virtue—the subordination of individual interest to the common good, which could not be coerced but would have to come from a recognition of the priority of the greater good of the community. This recognition was, in turn, a matter of individual conscience and good judgment. Considering the interests of others guaranteed that one's own interest would be recognized. It does not seem to me far-fetched to suggest that the health of educational institutions calls for the application of this concept of the public good and for the cultivation of the academic equivalent of these civic virtues.

This book provides a practical approach to academic management; it is not a philosophical treatise about academic government. Nevertheless, the approach it describes can help achieve greater community, civility, and common good within our academic institutions. McCorkle and Archibald have drawn intelligently on their own administrative experience and that of colleagues in other highly successful institutions. They have, in this sense, distilled collective wisdom about academic decision making. The result is worthy of thorough study and intelligent application by anyone with a serious interest in, and responsibility for, increasing institutional effectiveness. Quite apart from the merits of its specific suggestions, the book is valuable because of its basic assumptions. It assumes, with due regard for the uniqueness of educational institutions, that management is important, that there is a general body of knowledge about management that can be applied to such institutions, and that management skills can be learned. The higher education community has given only half-hearted support to these propositions. This book provides a serious opportunity both to consider their validity and to apply them on the basis of effective experience.

July 1982   Roger W. Heyns
                                                    President
                          The William and Flora Hewlett Foundation

❧❧❧ Preface

Great universities have gained prominence because of the high quality of students and faculties, environments conducive to scholarly endeavor, and the contributions and financial support of their constituencies. Although the initiative of farsighted administrators has helped ensure greatness, sophisticated management alone did not produce it. Now, given enrollment problems, inflation, financial stress, inflexibly committed resources, and increased political pressures, colleges and universities must be well managed if they are to remain great and, in many cases, their leaders will need to change their attitudes toward management—as well as their managerial styles—if they are to foster needed academic change and renewed institutional vitality.

We have written this book to show how new approaches to academic management can meet the needs of the 1980s. We present a tested model for management based on the best administrative practices currently in use within higher education as well as on proven methods from outside higher education that can be adapted to college and university management.

Our objective is to help academic administrators at all levels gain a better understanding of the challenges facing higher education and the means by which these challenges can best be turned into opportunities. We also aim to help trustees and state officials who govern, provide funds for, and establish public policy for higher education, as well as faculty members who, beyond their teaching and research responsibilities, find themselves increasingly called on to assist in the management of their institutions.

Origins of This Book

Our theme is that colleges and universities must modify their management practices if they are to retain academic quality and intellectual vitality in the face of predicted enrollment decline and increasing financial stringency. Out of efforts to improve management in the University of California system, by 1978 we had conceptualized what we believed to be a theoretically sound management model to meet the challenges ahead and had tested its major elements empirically in that setting. Because this approach to management appeared to be increasingly valid in providing useful results within a nine-campus system, we felt it had potential for broader application. We chose first, however, to analyze both the management theories on which it is based and its applicability to other institutions by comparing it with management practices in other leading universities across the country. We selected ten such institutions for examination on the basis of their geographic locations, their forms of governance (public or private), and the nature of their management organizations. The six public universities that we visited were the universities of Michigan, Minnesota, Missouri, North Carolina, Texas, and Wisconsin. The four private universities were the University of Chicago, Columbia University, Cornell University (partly private and partly public), and Stanford University. We interviewed over 120 administrators and faculty members at these institutions. In multicampus systems, we conducted interviews on at least one major campus in addition to the system headquarters.

This research permitted us to assess the past and planned management decisions of these institutions as well as their decision processes in the context of the model we had developed. The interviews also gave us an opportunity to learn how presidents, faculty leaders, vice-presidents, budget officers, and other administrators view present and future challenges confronting their institutions, thus providing verification of our assumptions underlying the need for improved management and a critique of our University of California experience. On the basis of these on-site visits—as well as of a review of the extensive literature on planning, governance, organizational behavior, budgeting, financial management, evaluation, and administrative control and strategy—we refined and extended our model and our interpretation of its applicability.

The management concepts, processes, and style that we advocate are applicable to a wide range of institutions. Community colleges can incorporate our ideas, as can the most complex graduate research universities, whether public or private. Each of the more than 3,000 higher education institutions in the United States is unique in its problems, its resources, its environment, and its opportunities; hence, we cannot prescribe specific application of our concepts for every institution. Improved management is possible in all of them, however, through the creative adaptation of these concepts by leaders who understand and respect their institutions' uniqueness. Our book is dedicated to improving academic management.

Content of the Book

During the remainder of the 1980s, American colleges and universities will need to meet at least eight challenges if they are to carry out their essential activities of instruction and research effectively. Chapter One describes these challenges: (1) protecting and enhancing institutional quality, (2) maintaining financial viability and independence, (3) keeping essential personnel and facilities vital in the face of few, if any, additions, (4) increasing student participation and improving access to higher education, (5) enhancing operational efficiency and productivity, (6) improving public understanding and support, (7) learning to live more effectively with uncertainty, and (8) developing and implementing management processes that are adapted to the academic setting.

Higher education has traditionally deemphasized the need for management, and academicians assuming administrative posts have rarely had formal management training or experience. Given this attitude toward management and the limited administrative experience of most academic leaders, it is understandable that current academic management practices are often inadequate to handle successfully the challenges facing higher education. But it is also difficult to gain acceptance for the fact that significant revamping of existing management practices is needed. Thus, in Chapters Two through Nine we analyze the weaknesses of traditional academic management and present a systematic and practical approach to management that is consistent with academic values and decision-making structures. These chapters show how to integrate the three primary management functions of planning, managing resources, and assessing results.

Chapters Two through Four show how to undertake *planning,* which is defined as setting objectives and selecting steps to attain them by analyzing and evaluating alternatives in the context of the opportunities—and constraints—that can be foreseen. Next, Chapters Five through Seven explain *resource management,* that is, selecting the best course of action and carrying it out through the acquisition and allocation of all types of resources—human, financial, space, time—and setting necessary policy guidelines and controls on their use. Chapters Eight and Nine then describe *assessment of results,* which means comparing the outcome of the implementation process with planned objectives to determine the degree of their achievement, reasons for any variation, and needed corrective actions.

Many administrators are discouraged from making necessary changes in management methods because of general institutional inertia and apprehension about change, combined with the continuing attitude of many faculty members that administration encroaches on faculty prerogatives. Most leaders who opt for change adopt an incrementalist approach to introducing new processes. This is appropriate if the increments are carefully planned and coordinated. When they are not well planned and sequenced, however, leaders appear to be "muddling through" rather than taking positive steps to improve management. Chapter Ten provides guidance for such an improvement effort. It examines the pragmatic aspects of implementing new management practices in colleges and universities through leadership strategy and understanding the politics of change.

Acknowledgments

Our suggestions and analysis are based on the collective experience and wisdom of many administrators and scholars, and we wish to acknowledge the contribution to our thinking of the faculty leaders and administrative officers at the institutions we visited and elsewhere who shared with us their plans, aspirations, and frustrations during the course of our study. Their experiences strongly encouraged us to present the case for better management in higher education.

It has been possible to produce this book because of the generous support provided by a study grant from the Ford Foundation, by Warren Mooney through the California Aggie Alumni Foundation, and the Department of Agricultural Economics, University of California, Davis. The encouragement offered by Fred Crossland, Emil Mrak, and Frank M. Bowen has been equally important. JB Lon Hefferlin of the California Postsecondary Education Commission provided extensive advice and assistance throughout the project. His editorial contributions and critical review were invaluable.

We are especially indebted to President Emeritus Charles J. Hitch, who, as president of the University of California, understood the need for improved management and provided the opportunity and continued support to develop many of the ideas put forth in this volume. The chancellors of the nine campuses of the university must be recognized for their sometimes critical but always constructive advice and cooperation as they participated in the inception and development of the management approach presented here. The helpful suggestions and encouragement from many administrators and staff members on the nine campuses and in the university's central office contributed much to developing new directions in university planning and management. Many of the refinements are the result of extensive interchange with faculty members and administrators on the Davis campus of the university, and we wish to thank these colleagues, particularly those in the Department of Agricultural Economics, for their constant encouragement, patience, and tolerance. The clerical assistance provided by staff members of the department turned a difficult task into a pleasurable experience for us. Janice Aboytes, Beth Connelly, Cathy Grindheim, Julie Hamilton, and Jessica Woods cheerfully and consistently met tight deadlines; and Diane Branam and Pauline Lindsay deserve special acknowledgment and gratitude for their contributions throughout the project and for preparing and coordinating the final manuscript.

Davis, California   Chester O. McCorkle, Jr.
July 1982   Sandra Orr Archibald

༄ ༄ ༄ Contents

Part Two: Resource Management

Part Three: Evaluation

9. Applying Techniques for Evaluating Programs,
    Personnel, and Resource Use   165

10. Management and Leadership Strategies in Action   190

    Bibliographical Resources on Academic
    Management   212

    References   221

    Index   230

✒✒✒ The Authors

Chester O. McCorkle, Jr., is professor of agricultural economics and administration, University of California, Davis. Since 1952, his teaching and research career in the University of California has been interspersed with administrative appointments as dean of the College of Agricultural and Environmental Sciences and vice-chancellor of academic affairs (at Davis) and eight years as vice-president of the University of California nine-campus system. In the latter position, he served as chairman of the university's Academic Planning and Program Review Board and was responsible for operating and capital budgets and financial planning for the system. He also was principal spokesperson for the university before the state legislature on planning and budgetary matters and represented the university with the Federal Relations Council of the American Association of Universities and the California Postsecondary Education Commission.

McCorkle's fields of interest include business organization and management, strategy and policy, and production economics. Numerous domestic and foreign consultancies include service on the National Research Council's Commission on Natural Resources, chairmanship of its Board on Agriculture and Renewable Resources, and chairman of studies relating to agricultural trends and productivity. He served on the staff of the Center for Economic Research in Athens and as a technical consultant in agricultural development in Chile and Argentina. His current research emphasizes factors affecting productivity of American agriculture, including changes in the physical resource base and its use, regulation of inputs, assumption of risk, and the financial structure of agricultural firms. He is the author of more than 100 articles, papers, and books. His research activities have been supported by grants from the U.S. Department of Agriculture, the Ford Foundation, the National Academy of Sciences, and the Agricultural Development Council.

He has served on the editorial board for the *American Journal of Agricultural Economics,* as president of the Western Agricultural Economics Association, and on the board of directors of Universal Foods and Del Monte Corporation. He has received numerous awards for research, teaching, and professional services, including Professor of the Year at University of California, Davis; Alumnus of the Year Award from California State Polytechnic University; and Distinguished Service Award from the University of Redlands.

He received his bachelor's and master's degrees from the University of California, Berkeley (1947 and 1948, respectively) and his doctoral degree in agricultural economics from the University of California, Berkeley (1952).

Sandra Orr Archibald is a postgraduate research economist in the Department of Agricultural Economics, University of California, Davis.

Her professional experience spans ten years in the University of California systemwide administration, including five years in the budget office, where she was responsible for long-range academic/budgetary planning and special studies in budgetary management. After completing assignments related to improving information systems and systemwide institutional organization in the university, she served for eighteen months as special assistant for resource management policy and methodology.

At the national level, she was director of economic analysis for the Rockefeller Commission on Critical Choices for Americans, examining questions of long-range national planning policy and resource allocation. She consulted to former Vice-President Nelson Rockefeller and to the U.S. Environmental Protection Agency on research planning and budgeting systems. Since 1980 she has been a consultant to a committee of the National Research Council, National Academy of Science, examining technical, economic, and social trends in American agriculture.

Her research interests center on public policy analysis, particularly as it affects agricultural productivity, and developing and applying quantitative methodology. Having authored several articles on budgeting and planning in higher education, Archibald retains a strong professional interest in college and university management.

Archibald received her bachelor of arts degree in 1967 and her master of public policy degree in 1971 from the University of California, Berkeley. She also holds a master of science degree in agricultural economics and is nearing completion of her doctoral degree in the same field at the University of California, Davis. Her research explores how environmental regulation influences decisions by agricultural firms and the consequences of such regulation for productivity growth in American agriculture.

To the next generation
of university students—
Alison, Bryan, Dan, Jay, and Timothy

Management and Leadership in Higher Education

Applying Modern Techniques of Planning, Resource Management, and Evaluation

1

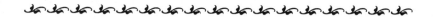

Challenges
Confronting
Management

By and large, American colleges and universities successfully met the challenges of growth in the 1950s and 1960s. Most of them "muddled through" the transitional 1970s, although some failed to survive. In the 1980s, fundamental changes in the character of American society, including its population, economy, and politics, are bringing fewer students, tighter budgets, and increased governmental intervention to higher education. These conditions present different challenges to administrators and faculty than did the conditions of the 1960s and 1970s. Academic leaders differ in outlook and perspective about how higher education will fare in the remainder of the 1980s, and circumstances affecting individual colleges and universities vary widely, but one fact is clear: Management will be challenged and tested on different issues and against different standards than it was during the decades of expansion.

1

The Postwar "Golden Age" of Higher Education

The twenty-five years between 1946 and 1970 have been called the most creative period in the history of higher education in the United States (Pusey, 1978). Following World War II, American colleges and universities passed through a quarter century of unprecedented enrollment growth spurred by expansion in technology, a strong economy at home and abroad, and a public attitude that encouraged and nurtured learning. Enrollments from 1946 to 1970 increased fivefold, from 1.7 million to 8.6 million—a rate of increase ten times greater than that of the general population. Faculty numbers increased nearly proportionately. Aggregate research budgets in higher education grew more than twenty times, from under $100 million to over $2 billion, while current expenditures rose by more than ten times in real dollars (National Center for Education Statistics, 1978, 1979), leading some to name these years the "golden age" of higher education.

Enrollments continued to climb during much of the decade of the 1970s, but the rate of growth dropped, and many campuses experienced substantial declines by the 1980s. In the face of competing economic and social priorities combined with high levels of inflation, real dollar expenditures for current operations per student fell by almost 20 percent during the 1970s, signaling to some the approaching end of the golden age.

David Henry, in *Challenges Past, Challenges Present* (1975), contends that there never was a golden age and that the challenges now so apparent were always there but were merely masked by the seemingly endless growth and unprecedented inflow of new money. Another college president has likened the "discovery" of challenges to islands emerging in a reservoir as the water level declined—always present but covered as long as the water remained sufficiently high.

Whether "golden" or not, the postwar era in higher education has come to an end. One distinguished university president recently looked at the 1980s and talked of the need for a "theory of bad options." Another commented that he "foresaw no pressing problems less money would solve." Few, if any, academic administrators believe they were dealing effectively—and fewer gracefully—with the effects of fundamental changes in our population, economy, and politics on our colleges and universities.

Future Constraints

Perhaps the most critical of these changed conditions is the substantial reduction in the traditional college-age population and the impact it is having on enrollments and finances in higher education. By 1992, the United States will have over 25 percent fewer eighteen-year-olds (National Center for Education Statistics, 1980). The impact of the decline in eighteen- to twenty-four-year-olds—the traditional pool—cannot be totally offset for all institutions by new programs, more active recruitment, and increased numbers of women, ethnic minorities, and older and part-time students.

Differential regional growth patterns make conclusions about individual institutional enrollment trends impossible. The number of public high school graduates in the Northeast region, for example, is projected to decline by 38 percent by 1990. Even within regions, variation among states is striking. In the West, California high school graduates are expected to decline by 24 percent, whereas those in Wyoming may increase by 21 percent and in Utah by 12 percent (Western Interstate Commission for Higher Education, 1979). Prestigious private and public institutions are less likely to be adversely affected by slowed or declining rates of growth than less well-known institutions; yet the popular disclaimer among administrators that "it will happen to everybody but us" is a classic example of the triumph of the academic mind over reality. Predictably, reality is emerging the victor.

Stringent financial conditions also mark a significant change from past decades when new money came nearly automatically, through appropriation or tuition, with annual growth in student numbers. Student expenditures in real dollars have continued to decline in the past several years. All but a few select colleges and universities have encountered serious financial constraints. Most are taking action to stabilize their financial position as best they can. For the first time many state institutions are being required to return a portion of their appropriated funds to the state during the current operating period, even when the appropriation is lower in real terms than that of the previous years. In fact, it is now highly likely that appropriations to higher education in many states will be reduced significantly, requiring major internal adjustments in program priorities. Public institutions either institute or raise tuition to partially offset declining appropriations. Private institutions continue to raise tuition in their attempt to meet rising costs, ever fearful of the effect higher tuition will have on enrollment. Declining federal appropriations for programs that provide funding for higher education, both public and private, are making the task of balancing current budgets ever harder.

Public universities are turning to the private sector for more money, just as private universities are seeking additional ways of obtaining more public funds (Breneman and Finn, 1978). All institutions are being forced to make better use of current resources. But despite present efforts, both public and private institutions will continue to have serious difficulty keeping pace with rising costs per student, and experience indicates that not all institutions will survive the 1980s.

In its final report, the Carnegie Council on Policy Studies in Higher Education advocated that "it is better to plan to meet the future effectively than just to fear it as a new dark age" (1980, p. 8). Understanding the challenges ahead is a first essential step in this process. Eight seem most urgent: protecting and enhancing institutional quality; maintaining financial viability and independence; maintaining the vitality of essential resources —faculty, management, staff, libraries, physical plant—in the face of few, if any, new additions to personnel or facilities; increasing participation rates and improving access of underrepresented students; improving operational efficiency and productivity; improving external understanding and support; learning to live more effectively and comfortably with the uncertainties that are likely to prevail into the indefinite future; and, above all, developing and implementing improved management processes of planning, resource management, and assessment, in order to accomplish the seven other tasks.

Protecting and Enhancing Institutional Quality

Our academic institutions stood the tests of the decades of expansion successfully but not without qualitative consequences. Administrators, responding to stimuli of growth, were occupied with constructing buildings, hiring faculty members, equipping laboratories, accumulating library collections, assimilating new monies, and processing students in ever-increasing numbers. Faculty members were hired and promoted to tenure ranks in numbers and proportions previously unknown in order to staff programs created to meet virtually all student demands. Program and resource distortions created by differential growth were regarded as short-term and correctable by additional resources expected in coming years. In research institutions, externally funded research increased to proportions requiring new or expanded administrative functions to support contract and grant activity. More professionals, such as student personnel administrators, accountants, and architects, quickly expanded the scope of management. New public service programs mushroomed on most campuses in response to requests from a broad range of constituents.

Few would argue that higher education was anything but stronger and more vital than at any other time in the nation's history. Leadership invested as wisely as time and resources permitted in achieving academic program quality; yet the quantitative aspects of growth were simply overwhelming. When growth slowed before most academic leaders expected, many campuses were left with unrealized and often unrealistic institutional aspirations with respect to academic programs, only marginally adequate funding for these programs, and imbalances in programs and faculty talents, particularly where commitments had been made to expand a limited and special-purpose institution into a complete research university. Tightened resources brought serious inequities in faculty workloads, excessive numbers of either very large classes or classes too small to be economically viable, and deterioration in the physical plant and instructional equipment. In programs with declining enrollments, underemployed faculty members have grown apprehensive, morale has declined, and the quality of teaching and scholarship has been impaired.

The definition of quality varies widely among institutions, but most faculty and administrators know which programs at their institutions are of high and low quality. They would most likely agree that quality is unlikely to be found in fragmented course sequences, overcrowded classrooms, or badly maintained buildings; and they would espouse the over-arching objective of protecting and enhancing educational quality. But looking ahead, achieving quality will mean attaining a number of subobjectives or goals in the face of highly constrained resources. Programs will need to match institutional mission; the quality of program offerings will need to be assessed; and priorities will need to be set for allocating and reallocating limited resources among them.

Faculty members will be challenged to provide expertise in evaluating program quality, weighing program priorities, and advising on necessary corrective actions. Only faculty members can provide this needed academic judgment, but candid, disinterested, and impartial advice about the reallocation of resources will not come easily when the result may be termination of colleagues in programs judged dispensable. Most difficult for faculty and administrators alike to accept may be that their institution *must* shrink in size to retain quality and stature.

Maintaining Financial Viability and Independence

Colleges and universities have never had sufficient resources to meet *all* the objectives of their faculties and administrators, but as the growth in resources going to higher education has slowed in recent years, they have had increased difficulty meeting even existing program obligations. The performance of the economy has severely affected levels and sources of funds for higher education. A decade of serious inflation has weakened many private institutions, dependent as they are on endowment income and capital gain, and its impact on public institutions has been compounded by economic recession and declining tax revenues, which have decreased the funds available for them. During the past ten years, as endowment income has dropped sharply as a relative contributor to total operating budgets (National Association of College and University Business Officers, 1978), the private sector has had to place greater reliance on tuition to meet operating and other costs. Tuition and fees in private institutions now provide well over one third of total current fund revenue (Leslie, 1979). So far, both public and private institutions have been able to increase tuition without adversely affecting enrollment by expanding student financial aid, largely with funds from the federal government, which at the end of the 1970s was providing over $6 billion annually for student aid (U.S. Office of Education, 1979). Publicly supported financial aid is extremely critical to the financial health of private colleges and universities, but it represents only one aspect of a broad, though at times subtle, shift toward their increased reliance on government for financial support.

At the same time, private giving by individuals, foundations, and industry, which had long provided operating funds and needed capital facilities for private institutions, has become increasingly important for public colleges and universities, not merely for providing a "margin of excellence" beyond state appropriations but as an important source of core support. As a result, both public and private institutions are increasing their development, or fund-raising, activities for gifts, bequests, and nongovernment grants.

The drop in spending for research and development and for basic research as a fraction of the federal budget over the past decade has represented another significant change in the financing of higher education. Although research funding is still large, more than half of federal research funds go for military purposes, and an increasing portion is devoted to applied rather than basic research (U.S. National Science Foundation, 1979b).

Looking ahead, a strong economy will be necessary, but not sufficient, to guarantee high levels of support to higher education. Tax and spending limitations are severely curtailing appropriations, and defense spending and the demands of an aging population will continue to be strong contenders for available dollars. Since government funding formulas typically link appropriations to enrollments, the decline in the traditional college-age population will make it easier for state and federal budgeters to redirect resources away from higher education. One challenge to administrators will be to reduce the influence of enrollments in determining appropriations. A second will be to convince funders of the shortsightedness of cutting public funding for education, since a technologically advanced society such as ours cannot be content with educating only a small portion of its population; and in times of slow economic growth, the best investment that society can make is in educating an ever greater proportion of its population and encouraging research that will enhance growth, increase productivity, and improve the quality of life (Bowen, 1977).

College and university administrators will likewise be challenged to maintain necessary institutional independence by resisting excessive regulation, oversight, and intrusion that may accompany funds, whether from government, industry, or individuals. Faculty will be challenged to protect program quality in the face of strong financial incentives to lower standards in order to maintain enrollments.

Keeping Human and Physical Resources Vital

The intellectual vitality of a university or college depends almost entirely on the interests and enthusiasm of its faculty. During the era of growth, each year added vitality to the campus—new people, new ideas, new courses, and new programs. Growth meant more funding and facilities as well, and all combined to create vitality. Presidents and chancellors have now recognized that, with slower growth, alternative means of providing for essential vitality must be found. Because colleges and universities added unprecedented numbers of young faculty members over a relatively short span of years, they will see few retirements during the next decade. In some institutions, annual retirements are now less than 1 percent of the faculty, and in a large number of programs no turnover will occur for a decade. Under financial stringency, the typical short-run administrative responses to slower growth have been those easiest to institute but also likely to complicate achieving academic vitality in the future—those of terminating nontenured and, therefore, younger faculty members and adopting a "revolving-door policy" to avoid future long-term commitments, thus effectively shutting out the major source of new academic skills and ideas. The intellectual problems of an aging, stable, and tenured faculty must be faced and resolved.

The same need exists for assuring continued vitality among academic administrators. The infusion of new ideas and vigor in management is as crucial as in academic programs. Not only do people grow stale in administrative assignments, particularly in more difficult and taxing ones, but many current administrators who grew up with growth and expansion find today's management issues more frightening and frustrating than challenging.

With few exceptions, physical plants show serious signs of neglect, and further deferral of maintenance and postponement of equipment purchases will only mean much larger expenditures in the future. Administrators must not only meet mandated requirements for accessibility and safety of structures but provide attractive, clean space to meet new as well as continuing academic needs. Finding funds to accomplish major capital renovation is going to be a most difficult challenge.

Maintaining financial flexibility contributes an important dimension to the vitality of human and physical resources. Not only are internal controls over resource use sharply reducing financial flexibility as the growth of funding has slowed, but many institutions have committed funds to programs into the indefinite future without retaining liquidity for instituting future program changes. Some have spent financial reserves in the short run to meet existing program commitments—and have postponed difficult choices among programs. These same choices will be faced in the coming years, when they will be no easier to make, and the loss of further flexibility will make their implementation even more difficult.

Administrators must find means of assuring institutional vitality through new ideas and new programs without significant new money. They will be challenged to improve personnel management and develop more opportunities for in-service faculty and staff growth than in the past. Faculty members must actively seek out new concepts and knowledge rather than rely on new colleagues to bring new ideas with them to academic programs at the beginning of every year. Above all, chief executives must keep management skills current and active. The price of "old, tired, and uninspired" leadership, to quote a former university president, is too high.

Increasing Participation Rates and Improving Access

The number of students enrolling in higher education depends to a large degree on demographic factors, economic conditions, and public and institutional policy. In the past, enrollment growth stemmed from both population growth and increased participation rates among high school graduates. Although the college-age population has slowed its growth and will soon decline, there remains room for improvement in participation rates, particularly among ethnic minority and low-income students, women, and older adults. Looking ahead, faculty and administrators will be challenged to increase the participation rates of all potential students but particularly of students from these historically underrepresented groups. In doing so, they will be challenged to uphold acceptably active recruiting against overly zealous recruitment that would be a disservice to students as well as harm the long-run interests of their institution. Faculty, administrators, and students can help seek out able high school and junior high school youth whose backgrounds have not been conducive to pursuit of academic goals and encourage them to prepare for college. Faculty will then need the ability to instruct students from a wider range of backgrounds and with more disparate levels of preparation than in the past—and to do so without diluting the standards of achievement that are essential to high-quality academic programs. The balance between access and quality is a delicate one, and if it is not maintained in the classroom, it will not be maintained at all.

The nation is committed to removing cultural and economic barriers to college and university attendance by ethnic minority students. Further increases in the proportion of minority and low-income youth enrolling can be achieved as long as financial support is adequate, college attendance retains its economic value, and institutions provide the necessary support and counseling services.

The participation of women between ages eighteen and thirty-four in higher education rose sharply in the last decade, and women now constitute more than 50 percent of all college students. Yet the rate at which women participate is still below that of men, and the rate of participation among women eligible to attend based on previous academic achievement is particularly low (U.S. Bureau of the Census, 1976). Gains are thus possible in women's enrollment. Further expansion of participation of older men and women is also feasible, given the growing need for midcareer retraining, the economic pressures on many women to reenter the job market, and the desire by many adults to enhance the quality of their lives through learning.

But many of these students will opt for part-time programs, which can impose disproportionate additional costs on institutions. Part-time students may use the library, health care facilities, and other student services as much as full-time students. They are also likely to be interested in different kinds of academic programs than students of traditional college age. To attract them, institutions will require financial flexibility to accommodate services and programs to their interests.

Enhancing Operational Efficiency and Increasing Productivity

Faculty time is the most important and expensive resource of any college or university. The challenge is to use it wisely. Higher education is labor-intensive in that salaries and employee benefits account for between 80 and 85 percent of typical institutional operating budgets. Therefore, if the educational quality of colleges and universities is to be maintained and enhanced in the face of declining real dollar budgets, improvements in efficiency and productivity must come from better use of their human resources.

Faculty productivity as measured by instructional output (student credit hours) per man-hour has shown little or no increase historically (O'Neill, 1971). Despite attempts to increase productivity using such techniques as television, computer-assisted instruction, and programmed self-study, there has been little substitution of capital for labor, although these methods have generally improved the quality of instruction. The current stringent budgets of some institutions are forcing increases in faculty productivity in terms of pushing classroom contact hours and teaching workloads in high-enrollment fields back toward 1950 levels—before the competition of the 1960s and 1970s for faculty led to reduced teaching assignments. But these increases in workload can reduce faculty members' effectiveness, since they may reduce faculty members' ability to remain current in their fields, to offer quality instruction, to conduct significant research, and to perform creative public service.

The effectiveness of faculty in these three traditional responsibilities is being adversely affected by time-consuming involvement in institutional administration as well as new reporting and accountability requirements for personnel administration, student recordkeeping, and research grants. Money to provide support services to aid faculty in meeting these new requirements not only has been inadequate but in institutions facing budget stringencies has been a prime target for cost savings, thus placing further burdens on faculty time. An increasing challenge is, therefore, to achieve a higher level of efficiency in all supporting services. Only by this means can faculty members be relieved of such tasks as answering telephones, filing, recordkeeping, and photocopying in order to increase their productivity in teaching, research, and service.

Improving External Understanding and Support

Historically, American colleges and universities have benefited from their partnership with other major institutions of society—economic, cultural, and governmental. Their post–World

War II growth was underwritten by broad support and consensus among these constituencies. This consensus deteriorated sharply in the late 1960s as increasing numbers of students questioned college and university ties with business and government, and many legislators and benefactors questioned faculty attitudes toward student unrest. Greater government regulation and detailed reporting requirements evidenced distrust and misunderstanding by state and federal officials. Increases in government appropriations were matched with increased oversight and questioning both of program objectives and of resource use. Threats of withholding money became a tool of legislators and government agencies to obtain compliance with their objectives. Attachment of policy language to appropriation bills required specific actions to be taken and limited the use of funds, but by failing to challenge such regulation for fear of greater retaliation, institutions invited increasing legislative intrusion through the budget process. What had been a partnership between government and academic institutions deteriorated to an adversarial relationship.

Without mutual understanding and respect, pressures for greater regulation will increase. Administrators, faculty representatives, and student leaders, both individually and through their state and national organizations, are learning to engage in external political activity more effectively and are giving more attention to effective representation of their positions at both state and national levels. Governing boards will likely make increased use of the courts to protect against incursions into internal affairs by external groups. But higher education officials must work even harder to improve their relations with institutional constituencies and particularly with federal and state governments. Administrators and faculty will be challenged to develop satisfactory techniques for achieving self-imposed institutional accountability as a substitute for externally imposed reporting requirements and controls. Administrators must show that they do not oppose legitimate government oversight but that overregulation lessens institutional flexibility essential to improve efficiency and productivity. Through improved management processes, they can help restore public confidence in institutional management and, ideally, lessen pressure for further governmental control.

Chief executive officers and governing board members will continue to have primary responsibility for reaching external constituencies, but they can no longer bear this burden alone. Faculty members will also be challenged to reach out with information and assistance to potential constituents and friends of higher education—groups too often neglected during the decades of growth and the years of student unrest.

Learning to Live with Uncertainty

For most of the postwar period of growth, the planning environment for higher education was fairly stable. Even when changes in funding, enrollments, and student interests fell outside expected ranges, slack in resources was usually sufficient to make adjustments relatively easy. Recently, however, levels of uncertainty have risen, and slack in funding to cushion unforeseen change is not available.

Unfortunately, continuing uncertainty and lack of flexibility are apt to damage faculty and student morale and institutional dynamism. Intellectual productivity and creativity could well decline, just when they are most needed to help institutions—and society—through what may be a most trying period.

In every institution, a good many faculty and administrators understand what actions are likely to be necessary if their institution is to retain academic quality and vitality. They are psychologically prepared to face enrollment and financial uncertainty realistically and with a degree of confidence. They recognize that the future will require different management techniques than traditional approaches have provided. But such equanimity is certainly not universal. Some faculty and administrators may be aware of increasing uncertainty but avoid its implications, perhaps fearful that if they engage in contingency planning, the contingencies will become self-fulfilling. Unprepared for action, they are likely to overreact in crisis with short-term palliatives that are not consonant with long-term institutional objectives. Farsighted institutional leaders will be challenged to help faculty prepare for uncertainty both through keeping them informed of trends affecting institutional operations and through involving them in discussions of alternatives for responding to these trends.

Developing and Implementing Improved Management Processes

College and university policy makers can increase the chances of successfully meeting the seven challenges just outlined if they adopt a management approach that consciously fosters academic change. Developing and pursuing such an approach will be the over-arching challenge of the remainder of the 1980s for academic administrators.

During growth, errors in administrative judgment were quickly corrected and seldom catastrophic. Annual budget increases covered administrative mistakes in the same way as the work of the landscape designer hides the less attractive creations of the architect. Now, the processes of management decision making on curricula, personnel, and the allocation of scarce resources in the vast majority of colleges and universities are inadequate to serve their needs. Planning staff, for example, are often isolated from faculty and administrative policy formulation. Management strategies to implement institutional objectives are difficult to identify. Resource management is predominantly budget-oriented and fund-based—inadequately tied to planning and assessment of the use of space, time, and human resources. And although the capability to evaluate the quality of academic programs is growing, comparable progress has not been made in assessing the impact of policy and resource decisions. Many academic administrators are unfamiliar with ways to adapt modern principles and practices of planning, resource management, and program assessment to academic institutions, either dismissing them, on the one hand, as inappropriate to the decentralized mode of shared governance characteristic of academic institutions or, on the other hand, using them in a style of central control that is neither appropriate nor necessary in colleges or universities.

Looking ahead, campus leaders can establish academic and financial planning processes, resource allocation procedures, and performance assessment techniques to assist in the attainment of institutional objectives. Different management can aid the maintenance of quality while minimizing the possibility of reducing budgets, terminating programs, and laying off faculty and staff. In the past, when faced with complex problems, administrators have often accepted simplified concepts and decision rules, such as across-the-board cuts in budgets and hiring freezes (Drucker, 1980). The challenge to academic administrators is to develop more sophisticated and defensible criteria for resource allocation than these "equal" but seldom equitable formulas. Faculty will be challenged to bring their critical academic perspective to planning and assessment, to provide timely counsel on fast-breaking problems, and to put professional and institutional obligations ahead of disciplinary and personal self-interest in rendering personally trying judgments on programs and colleagues.

Elements of Effective Management

The primary components of management adequate to meet the challenges facing academic institutions are planning, resource management, and assessment of results. These three basic management functions form a cycle—a sequence of management steps, transformations, and intellectual transactions conducted repeatedly over time to reach desired outcomes. As illustrated by Figure 1, in this cycle, the results of evaluation inform subsequent planning, which in turn affects resource decisions, which are then evaluated in terms of their results at the completion of the cycle. Plans will, of course, change, and resources will vary over time, but the management cycle, once correctly established, need not change. The three essential characteristics of the process are always present—dynamic, integrated, and iterative. They are dynamic in the sense that plans are viewed as "living" concepts, not as static blueprints that are updated every five years and left unchanged in the interim. Such static plans end up adorning bookshelves and desktops but not guiding management decisions. Planning, managing resources,

Figure 1. The Management Cycle

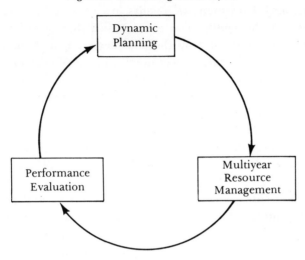

and assessing results are integrated in the sense that planning and assessment are both attitudes of management and a framework for thinking about and reaching day-to-day decisions. They do not exist "parallel" to an ongoing system of management, nor are they laid on top of existing practices. Instead, long-term strategic planning guides development of specific intermediate goals that can be transformed into multiyear resource plans and allocation decisions. The annual budget process —as important as it is, particularly to public institutions—is set in the broader context of resource acquisition and management. And assessing results is treated as an integral part of ongoing management activity, emphasizing flexibility to allow resources to be moved to new activities when needed.

Being dynamic and integrated, these three management functions are also iterative and not left to chance. Clearly stated and understood planning goals guide policy and resource use. Resource decision processes assure that plans are implemented. And both qualitative and quantitative assessment judges institutional effectiveness and efficiency in meeting planning goals and provides the basis for taking ongoing corrective planning and resource actions.

Many administrators and faculty would agree that man-

agement approaches that thus integrate planning, resource management, and assessment of results are critical to meeting the
challenges of the 1980s. The main reason that they have made
little progress in integrating these processes, apart from isolated
changes in administrative personnel and piecemeal changes in
planning, budgeting practices, and program review procedures,
has been the absence of clear means for linking long-term planning and annual budget making.

The major innovation of the approach to management described in the following chapters, compared with most traditional approaches to management, is its introduction of an
intermediate step between strategic planning and annual resource allocation in which long-term objectives and strategies
developed during the planning process are converted into defi-
nite multiyear goals and program plans to be realized in a "rolling" two- to three-year time period, and, at the same time, resource allocations are set in a context that transcends the annual
budget cycle. This approach both shortens the planning horizon
so that plans and priorities are made more realistic and concrete
and, at the same time, lengthens the resource allocation time
line beyond one year in order to provide more certainty and
sufficient lead time to adjust resources to achieve planned program changes.

We believe this approach to management offers major
hope to academic institutions in meeting their objectives and
the challenges confronting them. It helps replace the prevailing
resignation to "muddling through" and surviving year-to-year
with a sense of being able to influence the future and regain
some control over institutional destinies through logical incremental, or evolutionary, change. It gives full consideration to
the retention, protection, and enhancement of academic values
and to the complicated decision processes that set higher education institutions apart from most other organizations. It can be
conducted in a personal, informal, collegial manner that meets
the needs of faculty and administrators to reach consensus on
multiple objectives, allocate resources in light of them, and evaluate largely nonquantitative outcomes in an environment of
shared governance. Above all, it links the pieces of a compre-

hensive "systems" approach to academic management that are already emerging as college and university leaders struggle to make the difficult choices they face. It ties promising efforts at long-range planning for future program changes down to specific resource allocation and reallocation decisions. It feeds the results of excellent efforts to review the quality of academic programs back into operational decisions. It focuses the assessment of what has happened as a result of implementing past planning goals onto reconsideration of these goals and their implementation. And it provides the basis for developing information systems that provide useful data rather than unused printouts for assessing results, planning, and managing resources to meet the challenges ahead.

How these management concepts and processes as put forth in the following chapters can best be applied at any one institution will depend on the unique character of the institution and its leadership. It would be both inappropriate and a disservice for us to suggest homogenizing the rich diversity of American higher education through a prescriptive manual of standardized administrative procedures for adoption everywhere. Consequently, the remaining chapters emphasize the basic concepts and cycle of management that administrators can adapt in shaping the future of their institutions so that these institutions do more than merely survive. This active shaping of the future is the managerial imperative for higher education during the rest of the 1980s.

Current Planning
Practices and
Guidelines for
Improvement

Chapter One outlined the principal challenges facing colleges and universities in the 1980s and looked at the elements of academic management in light of how academic leaders can best approach these challenges. Given these challenges, the need for improved management processes is inescapable. The present chapter is the first of three that examine planning as the leading component of this improvement within the continuous cycle of planning, managing resources, and assessing results.

This chapter reviews the planning efforts of colleges and universities over the past twenty-five years; it reports how planning has been used during the last decade to come to grips with slower growth, financial stringency, and growing uncertainty; and it defines the planning needs of the 1980s and the dynamic character that planning requires if it is to meet these and other challenges. Next, Chapter Three presents a dynamic approach to planning that can guide colleges and universities in developing their own planning procedures. Chapter Four then offers an example of how this approach was actually implemented.

Planning During the Golden Age

Peterson (1980, p. 114) defines planning as "a conscious process by which an institution assesses its current state and the likely future condition of its environment, identifies possible future states for itself, and then develops organizational strategies, policies, and procedures for selecting and getting to one or more of them." Such planning is not new to higher education. Private colleges established in the American colonies were carefully planned, patterned predominantly after their antecedents in England. The land-grant colleges and universities so unique to the United States were founded to implement a series of national planning objectives—"to promote the liberal and practical education of the industrial classes in the several pursuits and professions of life"—thus positioning the country to feed, to clothe, and to house itself, to develop its resources and to engage in trade, and to prepare a cadre of reserve officers for military service in time of national emergency.

The planning objectives of higher education were equally clear after World War II: expansion to accommodate a rapidly growing number of students and, for graduate research universities, expansion of research and domestic and foreign service activities. New programs, new campuses, more professors, and new buildings were products of detailed "master plans" at both the institutional and statewide levels. And because it was nearly certain that any reasonable planning objective could be met, if not in this year, then in the next, rewards for planning were immediate and tangible. Continued economic and population growth, coupled with a strong public commitment to higher education, provided certainty and success to planning efforts.

The planning approaches of the growth era served adequately for those times and conditions. But they have not served a changed set of circumstances. Enough demographic information and analysis appeared by the late 1960s to raise serious question about future enrollment growth (Cartter, 1968). Yet many plans forecast a continuation of past growth trends long after these changes were well known. At least publicly, many colleges and universities held steadfast to earlier plans and projections. Certainly none publicly projected any future declines. Some administrators continued to believe that enrollment growth would remain strong. Others, however, so feared the financial stringency expected with enrollment decline that their institutional plans of continued growth often bordered on self-delusion. These plans became means of maintaining political postures, not useful tools to guide internal decisions or resource use.

State and federal officials reviewing public university and college budgets were not satisfied that these planning assumptions were realistic. Some of their doubts about the capabilities of public colleges and universities to plan were genuine concerns designed to encourage institutions to strengthen management practices in general and in particular to reevaluate and be more realistic in their planning assumptions about future growth and expansion. Others were, in part, tactical efforts designed to justify curbing what they foresaw as continually rising appropriations. Citing potential excess capacity in physical plants, destructive competition for students between institutions, unwarranted program duplication, and enrollment of more graduate students than traditional outlets could absorb as consequences of unchecked expansion and poor planning, government officials maintained that planning would have to be coordinated, if not controlled, by external agencies; they believed individual institutions were incapable of resolving these difficult issues with appropriate recognition of the "public good." As a result, statewide planning for higher education was expanded and eventually came to include private institutions as well as public when tightening resources and increasing competition for eligible students highlighted a new set of potential conflicts.

During the 1970s, college and university planning changed in both substance and form through a series of three stages, or periods. The first of the three, Stage One, sought to revise enrollment plans and control expansion of academic programs. The second sought fiscal control over restricted resources. The third and current stage seeks adaptability to continued enrollment and fiscal uncertainty. Not all institutions passed through these stages at the same time. In fact, some remain in Stage One, and many are yet in Stage Two.

Stage One: Planning for Slower Growth

The early 1970s might be considered a renaissance in planning efforts. Enrollment projections in most institutions were revised downward, often amid debate over what role enrollment assumptions should play in guiding program planning. Moratoria were placed on new programs; nevertheless, programs continued to be planned in the belief that they could be implemented in the near future. Administrators tried to discover and eliminate unwarranted program and course duplication, even though few courses were eliminated on the basis of redundancy, since whenever "overlap" was found, "uniqueness" was easily demonstrated. Concern arose over whether existing capacity in some program areas would exceed future needs, which led some institutions to use "manpower planning" as a means of controlling program size and guiding future program growth.

Except at a few institutions, however, the link between program planning and resource management was tenuous at best. Long-term planning tended to be ad hoc, focusing on specific proposals for new programs or specific policy issues. Even short-term planning was isolated from budget development. In many cases, "budgeting" set priorities that were not consistent with planning objectives. There seems to have been little understanding that planning objectives are accomplished primarily by carefully planned resource allocations over a period of time. As a result, Stage One planning was fundamentally static. It accepted "what was" as largely correct and projected it forward. Thus, projections of future resource needs, particularly for public institutions, were extrapolations of past student/faculty ratios, support dollars, dollars per student, and even administrative costs adjusted for inflation.

Efforts by professional planners in some institutions and state and interstate agencies to "quantify" higher education so that budgeting could be more directly tied to models of planning caused justifiable concern among faculty members who believed planners had vastly simplified notions of what academic institutions were all about if they judged institutional quality by reputational ratings and research quality, by the number of dollars or grants professors received, by the number of refereed journal articles they wrote, or by the frequency with which their writings were cited by other scholars. Little resulted from these well-intentioned but simplistic planning efforts except to generate opposition to academic planning in general and slow its evolution.

Another feature of Stage One planning was its emphasis on "formal" plans—formal in the sense that the "results" of planning should be published and available to all. This was, of course, a necessity for good professional planning; yet it generated further opposition. People could barely agree that enrollment was going to decline, let alone settle on numbers to appear in a public document. If they reached agreement on numbers, the figures inevitably were optimistically high. Thus, although publicity helped bring about acceptance of a slower growth rate —a major accomplishment in itself—the plans themselves were generally poor guides for subsequent management decisions. The governor of California commented that the academic plan of the University of California reminded him of a squid because it "squirted black ink" and did not point to a specific set of actions or decisions for the future. Yet, even convincing leaders of the university's campuses that they must change their expectations about the future size, program scope, and resources of their campuses was a significant accomplishment of the plan. Elsewhere, more was accomplished in this direction during this stage of planning than even such careful critics as Lee and Bowen (1975) recognized, since the critics failed to understand that long-term strategies and objectives, not just downward revisions on enrollment plans and curbs on further program expansion, had to be completed before more useful plans could be developed. This second stage was slow in appearing.

Stage Two: Planning for Financial Stringency

Stage Two planning during the late 1970s was stimulated by growing financial concerns. Stage One planning had helped change expectations about possibilities for program expansion, but the majority of institutions still did not realize the severity of their financial future. Private colleges and universities were beginning to meet operating costs by expending endowment corpus when costs ran ahead of expected revenues as a result of inflation and more sophisticated teaching and research activities. Major public universities began to feel the combined pressures of inflation, tightened appropriations, slower enrollment growth, and thus smaller increases in budgets.

By the middle 1970s, leaders of both public and private institutions recognized that resources were going to be constrained into the foreseeable future. Their plans had to reflect these constraints. Thus, Stage Two planning was characterized by greater realism and recognition by managers that the entire planning environment, rather than just enrollment pools, was changing. Planning was recognized as an ongoing management function. "Living within one's means" and assuring viability within expected resource levels became its chief responsibility.

New planning structures emerged in Stage Two. Planning "boards," "committees," and "work groups" were created to shepherd the planning process. Their duties varied from information gathering and analysis to advising the chief executive on programmatic issues to full review of academic and support program operations and advising on resource allocations. They found their assignments unfocused, difficult, and controversial, and their expectations of what they were supposed to accomplish generally exceeded their results. In several cases the only result of their work was a "plan to plan"—such as to establish a permanent planning committee. Yet a number of specific accomplishments were characteristic of Stage Two. As a first step, planning groups developed or revised institutional mission and objectives statements to provide a basis against which they could assess current activities, although in many cases this resulted merely in renewed commitments to "teaching," "research," and "public service" and to administrative disappointment that such statements were not of greater use in resource decisions. Second, planning groups sought to define a "core" academic program to gain a sense of desired program scope and to help set priorities for the future should resources be further constrained.

But the most universal planning activity of Stage Two was the review of academic programs. Many campus leaders and particularly graduate deans, concerned about the quality of some programs begun during the period of growth, were active in instituting reviews as a means of identifying strengths and weaknesses to guide future resource allocation decisions. In addition, external oversight groups, such as statewide coordinating bodies, promoted program reviews primarily to reduce unwarranted program overlap among institutions.

As a result, a number of programs were eliminated but with little significant cost savings. Faculty were usually absorbed into other programs or moved into administrative positions. Program development continued to be constrained; however, to attract new clienteles, some existing courses were packaged into new configurations. Proposals for genuinely new programs were studied carefully for resource implications, and some were approved with limited or no commitment for new resources. Joint planning between neighboring institutions increased in order to share expensive resources, such as faculty talent, library collections, and research facilities.

Personnel planning received added attention as administrators realized that faculty turnover rates were dropping to as low as 1 percent per year or lower and would remain at such levels for a number of years, and as they became aware of the possibility of having to terminate tenured faculty under financial exigency. Beyond consideration of faculty layoffs, some institutions began planning for a permanent reduction in faculty positions. One prestigious public university in the Midwest planned to phase in such reductions over a six- to eight-year period. The University of California imposed a policy requiring that 10 percent of "ladder rank" faculty positions be available for withdrawal within one year's advance notice.

Much formal and informal education of constituents took place during Stage Two, not only to raise their level of understanding about major planning problems but also to impart a sense of need for improved resource management processes. Indeed, the most progress in planning was evident at those institutions whose leaders spent a great deal of effort to inform benefactors, trustees, faculty, and students about planning and resource questions. Yet the tendency of administrators to centralize decisions in stressful periods influenced the way planning developed during Stage Two and created tension between administrators and faculty over their roles in the planning process. Each recognized the legitimacy of, and need for, the other's participation, but neither seemed to have resolved satisfactorily the question of "who plans."

Stage Three: Planning for Uncertainty

By 1980, most senior administrators and a growing proportion of faculty members were coming to accept the fact that enrollment and financial pressures were not going to subside. Consequently, they regarded the bounds that they had set on planning assumptions and implementing actions as too lenient. Recognizing that the future was truly different forced a fundamental change in managerial perspective and for the first time raised questions about the continuing viability of conventional administrative procedures. The most experienced administrators sensed the need to develop new management processes that better integrated planning with resource management. They also saw the need to assess the results of prior planning decisions as a basis for shaping future decisions. Such a process, they knew, could be developed only over time with extensive faculty consultation and careful experimentation.

Administrators knew, too, that no matter how obvious the problem and solution was to them, change in colleges and universities takes time to implement. Conflicting pressures and viewpoints surrounded every major choice.

Faculty members protect not only their prerogatives with respect to academic program decisions but the quality of the academic enterprise at large. Given the fuzzy boundaries that characterize shared governance on most campuses, planning presented an issue for debate about faculty and administrative prerogatives and responsibilities. The unsettled state of planning provided an attractive target for faculty criticism as well as an opportunity for faculty members to help define how their expertise could best be introduced into the management process.

In most colleges and universities, faculty creativity is so fertile as to be the source of almost unlimited ideas and ambitions for qualitative improvement. This is the essence of a healthy academic community that nurtures genuine intellectual growth. When it becomes less active, the vitality of the institution itself fades. The special role of academic planning for the 1980s is to provide an environment that fosters intellectual change and growth despite uncertainty. The strongest potential resource for change on a campus is a vital, well-informed, and involved faculty. Planning is the most promising means of engaging the faculty constructively in achieving change, but administrative leaders must set its direction and ensure its momentum to make it a useful management tool.

Need for Dynamic Planning

Given the rapid pace of change in higher education today, planning under uncertainty must be dynamic in outlook and style. Too often, as Drucker (1980, p. 4) has noted, "planning, as commonly practiced, assumes a high degree of continuity. Planning starts out, as a rule, with the trends of yesterday and projects them into the future—using a different 'mix' perhaps, but with very much the same elements and the same configuration." In a turbulent and not at all predictable time, when external events are likely to affect institutional decisions profoundly, planning cannot assume such continuity; it must anticipate what the greatest changes are likely to be and where they are likely to occur, and it can enable faculty and administrators to take advantage of new realities and to turn uncertainty into opportunity. Without planning, a good many colleges and some universities will be forced to close their doors (Cyert, 1978).

To meet the need for planning during the remainder of the 1980s requires more than public announcements that planning is going to be undertaken, reliance on professional planners to collect data, or the appointment of committees to issue ornate publications. Planning must be a frame of mind for administrators and faculty alike that provides a context for resource decisions and policy making at all levels of the institution. Above all, planning must be active. Static "blueprints" must be replaced with fluid sets of strategies designed to implement institutional objectives under various eventualities (Millett, 1977). With such strategies, academic leaders will be able to move quickly when opportunities arise, knowing that they have completed much-needed consultation and agreement on goals in advance.

Dynamic planning can not only help institutions adapt to external changes and improve their ability to acquire resources, it can make programs more efficient and effective in achieving institutional objectives and can improve morale and performance by fostering opportunities for individual growth (Peterson, 1980).

Our interviews with college and university administrators and faculty members have revealed strong support for improved planning but little evidence that many administrators know how to design or implement a dynamic planning process. At most institutions, administrators are still searching for a Stage Three approach to planning. Those who have searched for an appropriate planning mechanism have discovered that such planning requires changes in nearly all management processes, a task that many find most arduous. However, postponing the task only compounds the difficulty as internal opposition to any major management change intensifies as constraints increase.

What are the necessary characteristics of Stage Three planning? Despite the unique qualities, problems, and traditions of each institution, we believe that certain common elements must be present for planning to meet the uncertainties of the 1980s.

First, planning must support, not undermine, the complementary authority and responsibility of faculty and academic administrators at all levels. Most important personnel, resource, and academic program decisions are determined not by presidents or chancellors but by deans, department chairs, and faculty members. Planning for the 1980s must recognize this decentralized character of decision making in academic institutions and allow for the essential consultation and review that it involves. Because of the central role of faculty in shared governance, both faculty and administrators have long-term, or "strategic," planning responsibilities at each level of decision—department, division, and campus. In this way, colleges and universities differ from organizations where planning tends to center at the top. Chancellors or presidents can rarely make effective campuswide planning decisions without the advice of faculty members and deans, and the same holds true for all levels within the institution. If policy responsibility and authority are undermined or short-circuited in the planning process, implementation of plans will be stressful at best and perhaps impossible. Those responsible for implementing planning decisions can be far more effective and willing to carry them out when they have been included in discussions before decisions are reached.

Planning is so stressful when it involves consideration of eliminating programs and positions that mistrust and hostility are inevitable if decision processes are not impeccable. Realistically, conflict will arise over adverse decisions no matter how great the effort to build trust and confidence, but when faculty and administrators have confidence in the processes followed, their debate will focus on the substance of decisions rather than on procedures.

 Second, planning must establish and convey a sense of direction and purpose but not one of rigidity or inability to change in the face of new circumstances. New resources are no longer going to provide adequate flexibility to take advantage of unforeseen opportunities, and operating from static plans will not permit flexibility. For example, to adhere slavishly to a planned level of staffing in a particular department would be shortsighted if the department could unexpectedly attract a recognized expert in the field whose contribution could raise the department to a status of distinction. Planning must consider many alternative approaches to accomplishing institutional objectives and yet evaluate carefully their costs and consequences. In looking for more efficient ways of carrying out activities, analysts should guard that they do not sacrifice academic objectives or quality. Increasing class size excessively as a means of holding down faculty positions may reduce costs but also the quality of instruction. Cutting library hours will reduce expenses, but other changes, such as shared acquisitions, centralized bibliographical services, and off-site storage, can increase the quality of library service as well as reduce costs. Dynamic planning must substitute for growth as the means of applying resources to accomplish change by providing the direction and momentum for change.

Third, planning for change requires a substantial alteration in form and content of plans and planning. Descriptions of traditional forms and content of academic plans are available in a number of sources, such as Millett (1977) and Mayhew (1979).

Those institutions that will plan successfully for the rest of the 1980s will be those that avoid the temptation to create a traditional master "conceptual framework" or a large-scale "grand plan." Such plans have been encouraged by the ability of modern computers to collect, store, and manipulate data. These plans are seldom completed, and among those that are, many are so general that they do not identify achievable goals. In contrast, dynamic planning, as illustrated by Hussey (1979) and Quinn (1980), emphasizes completion of discrete manageable segments with managers coordinating the different segments for consistency and compatibility. In addition, rather than focusing on a particular time period, such as five or ten years, dynamic planning devotes attention to the different time periods during which plans can be implemented and constraints are operative. For example, the opportunities in the short run for altering the distribution of faculty talents on a campus are relatively fixed, whereas over a period of five years some opportunity exists for altering their distribution, and over twenty-five years an almost complete turnover in faculty talent will occur. Thus, major changes in faculty resources are highly constrained in the short term but become increasingly possible in the long term. Administrators who focus their attention primarily on making ad hoc short-term decisions regarding personnel without giving adequate attention to potential program needs ten or fifteen years away are perpetuating a pattern of eroding flexibility by small increments and making achievement of long-term planning objectives much more difficult.

Dynamic planning is also a process of negotiation and compromise. Many difficult planning decisions are best reached by frequent and informal face-to-face interchange among faculty and administrators. Such informal dimensions of planning must be understood and fostered. Persuasion is a powerful tool in planning. Informal discussion allows for tough debate to take place privately, the formal plan reflecting only the outcome. The classic "kitchen cabinet" of respected faculty leaders and key administrators provides one means for extensive informal exchange of ideas crucial for effective planning.

Fourth, college and university statements of objectives will remain relatively general and stable but must be translated into more specific goals to guide program and resource choices and must incorporate criteria against which results can be assessed. Even though general in tone, long-term objectives such as "the advancement of knowledge" or "improving academic quality" can carry great meaning for an institution if they are broken down into shorter-term intermediate goals that can be achieved through particular program choices and resource allocations. By being more specific, these more immediate goals can be used to assess the specific program resource needs and take action to implement them more effectively. In addition, assessment criteria need to be agreed on early as part of the planning process for goals to be effective guides to action. If they are not, debate over appropriate assessment will be never-ending. While quantitative benchmarks such as entering test scores of students, acceptance rates among admittees, academic performance, employment history, and professional contributions of graduates can provide important information to help in assessing the quality of academic programs, since outcomes are largely intangible, assessment must admit qualitative as well as quantitative information. Judgment, not reliance on quantitative data alone, must continue to play the more important role in such assessments.

Fifth, *planning assumptions need to be made explicit so that they can be assessed periodically for validity.* Since external events beyond the institution's control directly affect decisions, explicit evaluation of the external environment should be an ongoing planning activity. If assumptions in plans about external trends, such as demographic projections, are explicit, they can be examined and altered as needed. Some institutions even use changed demographic and workload assumptions to correct program imbalances and quality deficiencies that were products of past rapid growth. For instance, one reduced the size of its English department from more than sixty faculty members to fewer than forty over a relatively few years on this basis, while using this opportunity to define a core English program. Only careful planning and implementation with consistent vigilance for opportunities make possible a shift in program staffing of this magnitude.

Sixth, *planning must employ realistic short-term resource constraints and concentrate on those issues about which something can be done.* Imposing anticipated financial constraints on planning helps to ensure the necessary linkage of planning to resource allocations and policy decisions by making planning realistic. Resource constraints for annual or biennial budgets are well recognized but are sometimes neglected in drafting master plans and "grand designs." More effort should be made to plan and project resource "ranges"—the lower and upper bounds of resources likely to be available over the planning period. This will assure that realistic planning takes place and, at the same time, avoid overconstraint for future change.

If plans are to be useful and creditable guides to administrators and faculty, they must emphasize activities that the institution controls or can significantly influence. The Master Plan for Higher Education in California (Liaison Committee of the State Board of Education and the Regents of the University of California, 1960) has been effective for over twenty years because it dealt with broad segmental missions and specified enrollment pools for state higher education at a level of generality appropriate to the purpose it was designed to serve. Contrast this with an attempt by a system office to plan numbers of students by major and department for each of a number of diverse campuses. Even if the approach were valid, such plans are out of date before the ink is dry. Planning departmental size for the long term by projecting student interests from past trends, when students are free to choose majors and courses, is subject to serious question. The object of planning in this case is not controllable unless the institution decides to set upper limits on program size and limit student choice in the future. Even then, administrators can only cap programs, not control minimum size. However, a minimum academic core for a department consonant with academic objectives is a realistic and controllable planning goal. If the desire is to accommodate shifting student interests, then the plan should provide explicitly for the flexibility needed to augment various academic programs. Temporary allocations and deallocations can meet workload shifts. Permanent changes in human and financial resources should be consistent with planned core requirements.

   Seventh, the planning process must be in place before highly controversial and divisive issues must be faced. Planning is too often deferred while administrators solve current problems. Delay frequently results in options becoming more limited. Nearly all the college and university presidents we interviewed admitted that they began to develop planning processes too late. Of those forced to reduce expenditures within the past several years, none had had a plan ready for determining or implementing necessary cutbacks. All had initially resorted either to expedient across-the-board reductions or to retaining academic program budgets while reducing such support operations as physical plant maintenance. Most recognized that their lack of plans added to the trauma associated with reductions, threatened their credibility and effectiveness in dealing with their constituents, raised the likelihood of court challenges to faculty layoffs, and made subsequent adoption of planning processes even more difficult. Their concern about the "self-fulfilling" prophecy of planning for faculty reduction was rapidly disappearing as other institutions grappled with the issue and began to adopt guidelines for cutting back academic programs.

Since planning causes changes in the pattern of management within the campus, a concerted effort must be made to gain understanding for planning and prepare people from the outset and continue through the entire process. The human, or behavioral, side of planning is as critical to success as the technical aspects of the process (Cyert, Simon, and Trow, 1956; Miles and Snow, 1978). Unless much time and attention is given to raising the level of understanding of all those affected by decisions to come, it is unlikely that major changes can be accomplished without serious upheaval. Faculty involvement means more than being asked to respond to a completed proposal. Every major institution studied took nearly two years to gain the necessary level of faculty understanding before major changes were implemented successfully. Where such preparation was neglected, turmoil and conflict resulted—leading in some cases to replacement of senior administrators. Without preparation, the success rate of planning and its implementation is unimpressive.

Finally, key administrators must be committed to planning as a management tool. Defining problems, objectives, and goals and placing them in priority and perspective demand the commitment of core administrators and senior faculty members. As a minimum, presidents or chancellors must participate in shaping and articulating institutional objectives and consistently support and guide planning endeavors. In the absence of such leadership, efforts of administrative staff can become misdirected. Faculty then see planning as a staff activity and are less willing to participate in or accept planning decisions. In addition, influential outsiders, such as legislators and benefactors, begin to question the direction of the institution and the role of its administrative leaders. Without their primary involvement in planning, presidents and chancellors lose credibility and support. Their occasional planning statements, such as threats to curtail or close medical schools and other highly sensitive programs in the face of possible budget cuts, are seen as opportunistic and transparent.

Experienced administrators understand that participation in planning is a key responsibility, since planning is the key to institutional self-renewal and continual rejuvenation. As new fields of knowledge develop and interest in others ebbs, as faculty members grow older and retire, as buildings require remodeling or replacement, planning coordinates new programs, new faculty members, and new facilities. The increased uncertainties of the 1980s have not reduced the usefulness of planning. To the contrary, they have increased the need for planning and demonstrated its importance in the management cycle while at the same time complicating its task.

3

Dynamic Planning as a Primary Management Function

If colleges and universities are to turn adversity to opportunity in the turbulent 1980s, planning must be viewed as a management process with controlled change as its objective. It cannot be a separate activity conducted apart from other decision processes. Rather, it is integral, along with resource management and assessment of results, to the total management function. It must involve the ongoing translation of long-term institutional objectives into intermediate goals and multiyear resource plans. We therefore maintain that planning is both possible and a prime responsibility of administrators. We do not accept either the "political" model of academic government, which holds that plans and decisions emerge only through political power (Baldridge and others, 1978), or the "organized anarchy" approach (Cohen and March, 1974), which views academic institutions as consisting of a group of highly autonomous units where progress and change are best fostered by the professionals in each and planning is primarily a loosely coordinated process of allocating resources.

At the same time, in contrast to some planners, we advocate decentralizing planning to academic, administrative, and support units, thus avoiding either administrative overcentralization of this critical responsibility or its delegation to professional planners alone. This decentralization not only provides for informal exchange of information and suggestions among faculty, administrators, and staff (more, in fact, than is currently observed on most campuses) but also clarifies who makes decisions, when and where they are made, how they are reached, and the sequence in which they are made. Such planning calls for the give-and-take of "jawboning" that increases the information available for decisions, improves understanding, builds greater tolerance for the seeming ambiguity associated with many planning issues, recognizes the format in which most academic decisions are made, and reduces dependence on "standardized" data as the only approach to "impartial" analysis for decision making.

We also differ from some professional planners who maintain that all of the detailed substance and strategy essential to action must be contained in a formal planning statement or plan. We believe that senior administrators in any type of organization must avoid proposing some planned changes prematurely because of political complications that may then inhibit their accomplishment. Consequently, what administrators may approve for inclusion in a published planning statement may fall short of what most traditional professional staff planners believe to be essential to an operational plan. This difference of opinion reflects the different perspectives of administrators who are responsible for seeing that institutional objectives and goals are established and accomplished and administrative staff members who are responsible for assisting in the development of plans.

The basic elements in our approach to dynamic planning appear in Figure 2, which illustrates the planning activities of the management cycle and depicts their sequence and interrelationship. These activities are (1) evaluating current institutional objectives, strengths, and weaknesses and the external

Figure 2. Dynamic Planning.

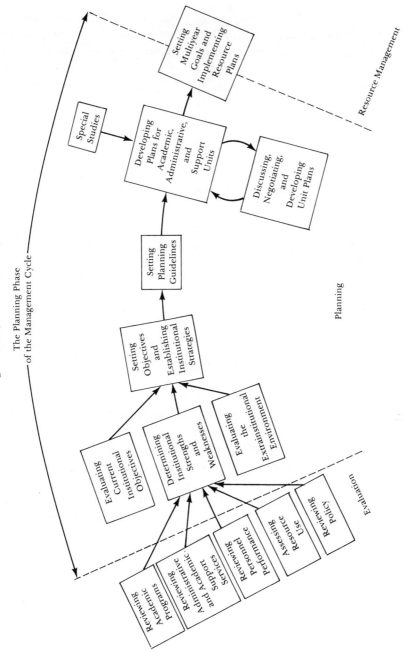

environment; (2) setting, reaffirming, or modifying institutional objectives and establishing broad strategies for reaching them; (3) establishing planning guidelines to direct preparation of unit strategic plans; (4) developing and integrating these strategic plans; and (5) developing multiyear goals and implementing resource plans to turn plans into action. Whatever structure and degree of formality an institution chooses for its planning process, the process must embody these five basic activities.

Evaluating Current Institutional Objectives, Strengths and Weaknesses, and the External Environment

Effective planning is grounded in an understanding of institutional values—what the institution seeks to do and should do—how well it accomplished these values, and the environment in which it operates. Much of this information comes from the assessment phase of the management cycle, to be discussed in Chapters Eight and Nine, including the review of programs, personnel performance, resource use, and policies.

Evaluating Current Objectives. Objectives—broad general statements of mission and scope—convey long-term program directions, areas of emphasis, and a sense of institutional character. They are largely qualitative and serve as the basis for specifying institutional goals and strategies. For example, one typical objective of most universities is to contribute to the advancement of knowledge. To do so, professors must stay at the forefront of their academic disciplines. Strategies typically instituted to implement this objective include sabbatical leave programs for all faculty members, special leave programs for individual faculty members, and travel funds for faculty participation in professional meetings.

Another typical university objective is to achieve excellence in academic programs. A goal to this end of excellence is to maintain flexibility in faculty resources in order to be able to add new faculty talent from time to time. Strategies to implement this goal of flexibility may include policies on the distribution of age and rank of faculty in various departments and divisions, mandated proportions of temporary appointees, and use of adjunct, visiting, and part-time faculty appointments where possible.

A third institutional objective may be efficiency in the use of resources. An intermediate goal to this end might be equitable distribution of resources to departments relative to their workload. Strategies to implement equity in resource allocation might include reallocating vacant faculty positions from departments with declining workloads to those with increasing loads and shifting funds for teaching assistants, secretarial staff, and other support services to departments with heavier workloads.

The objectives of colleges and universities differ from those of profit-making corporations in several respects that make their use in academic planning distinctive from that in business. Academic objectives typically are multifaceted and ambiguous. Disagreement exists about appropriate criteria with which to assess their attainment, in contrast to those of firms, where achievement during a given period of time can usually be measured against objective measures such as net profit, rate of return on equity, and change in the share of the market. The criteria for assessing attainment of academic objectives tend to be qualitative judgments rather than quantitative ones. And, in contrast to business and industry, where objectives are typically set by top managers and boards of directors, university objectives and the goals for achieving them are subject to continued debate by all institutional constituencies. Thus, academic leaders need to build consensus about objectives and goals through complicated and largely political processes regarding what the institution should be, in what direction it should move, and what it should accomplish; and, as a result, change in academic objectives occurs more slowly and incrementally.

Some academic administrators view evaluation of the adequacy or appropriateness of current institutional objectives as the principal, if not the sole, element in planning. It certainly is essential, but it is only the first step in the process of deciding on and implementing any change in direction. Peterson (1980) notes that in many cases it fails to provide even an adequate first step. For instance, if it produces only reaffirmation of "instruction, research, and public service" as institutional objectives, it offers little guidance for planning and none for setting new directions. Nonetheless, fundamental evaluation of the adequacy or worth of current objectives in light of social trends and societal needs should be a continuing process and a particular responsibility of the chief executive, working with key administrators, faculty, and the governing board. It allows a college or university to identify its special character, reaffirm its sense of purpose, identify targets of opportunity around which plans can be built, and make at least modest shifts in direction.

Determining Institutional Strengths and Weaknesses. The more thorough the review of strengths and weaknesses, the more realistic, and therefore useful, planning will be in serving administrators, faculty, and staff as they work to implement objectives. In fact, Hussey (1979, p. 14) argues that unless an organization "is willing to put itself under a form of self-analysis to assess its strong and weak points, it might as well give up the idea of planning."

Administrators of all colleges and universities periodically review the strong and weak points of academic and service units, instructional and research programs, and faculty and staff performance. But these reviews must be strengthened on most campuses in several ways to be useful for planning. They must be more consistent in their quality, their results must be available when needed, and these results must be analyzed by administrators with the assistance of faculty and staff in order to be integrated into the planning process.

One stumbling block to continual critical self-review on the part of administrative, academic, and service units in times of resource stringency is the knowledge that such review may result in changed priorities and resource reallocations. Another is lack of agreement on what is to be reviewed and what criteria or standards of performance should apply. But consensus on standards and on areas for review can improve markedly when it is evident that such information is actually considered in decision making!

Much of the most useful information in assessing strengths and weaknesses is not necessarily written. Academic deans, department chairs, and senior faculty members are good judges of the strong and weak points of academic and support programs and personnel. Senior administrators must consciously seek their judgments in assessing overall strengths and weaknesses. If deans, department chairs, and faculty members are included in the planning discussions, and if senior staff work closely with top administrators in synthesizing information from many sources as planning progresses, the process will naturally rely heavily on face-to-face discussions and not be dependent on written records alone. Many administrators, in our judgment, currently pay excessive attention in the planning process to formal written reviews containing large amounts of quantitative data and frequently prepared under the direction of professional planners without adequate direction from policy makers. This puts responsibility for assessing program strengths and weaknesses for purposes of planning in the wrong place, besides denying administrators a major source of knowledge and informed judgment about current program quality and potential. The importance of obtaining a balanced set of viewpoints in assessing strengths and weaknesses for planning cannot be overemphasized.

Evaluating the Extrainstitutional Environment. External forces shape institutional history and influence institutional decisions and management. Understanding both the opportunities and constraints these forces present will be increasingly critical during the rest of the 1980s. Administrators are forced to respond to changes in public attitudes toward higher education, as illustrated by the repercussions of the student disturbances of the 1960s and early 1970s. Even today, many faculty members and administrators have not been able to escape the sensitivities and cautiousness developed during this period, and they are unduly fearful of criticism.

The financial resources available to colleges and universities also constrain management as well as provide opportunities for change. Growth or decline in local and regional college-age populations and national economic trends obviously affect these resources, but other factors, such as the increasing mean age of the population or the decision to strengthen the nation's military capability, also have an indirect effect on resources available. In recent years, expanded financial aid has made both public and private institutions more dependent on public funding and has also drawn them more deeply into the political process.

Some observers argue that extrainstitutional forces are sufficiently beyond the influence of institutions that little reason exists to develop sophisticated environmental assessment (see Baldridge and others, 1978). We believe this perspective underemphasizes the ability of colleges and universities to affect these forces as well as the contribution that good management can make toward anticipating and preparing to respond to them. By evaluating the environment, the chief executive uncovers issues that are likely to be critical in setting and modifying objectives and establishing goals and planning guidelines. The consideration of such matters as trends in eligibility pools, potential clientele, financial support, and the political climate must be a primary responsibility of the chief executive, using information obtained from a wide range of sources—liaison officers with various external groups, such as government, alumni, community, and parents; institutional research staff; professional associations; and the informal network that administrators cultivate with their counterparts in other institutions, government, and business. Although an effective information base is broad and diverse, the task of synthesizing this information and interpreting its significance for planning decisions falls on the chief executive. For example, a staff analyst may detect the potential financial impact of a legislative bill, but unless the president and his or her immediate advisers then take action on the basis of this information, either to influence passage of the bill or to plan internal adjustments in the event that it passes, the president is not fulfilling a key duty of the presidency. If changes in planning assumptions are necessary, it is the chief executive's responsibility to articulate them to the academic community. It is this critical role in planning that requires presidents and chancellors to avoid being inundated with current crises, to reserve ample time for thoughtful reflection on events and emerging issues in the broader society, to read and converse widely, and to be able to delegate to others the conduct of much of operational administration.

Setting Objectives and Establishing Strategies

As noted earlier, college and university objectives seldom change radically in a short time. But strategies and short-range goals to achieve these objectives do change with circumstances. Objectives set broad institutional directions, ideals, and ideology. Their power stems not from their specificity but from the fact that they provide guidance for coherence and consistency among all short-term goals.

Strategic planning proceeds from the review of current objectives and agreement on any possible changes in them to determine how they can best be achieved over a realistic period of time, given assessment of the external environment and of institutional strengths and weaknesses. Traditionally, planning has relied on long-term objectives to project specific planning targets into the future. This procedure is not useful when environmental parameters are unstable. In such times, static projections of where institutions want to be in the future should be replaced with more realistic strategies that indicate how institutions can achieve their objectives by taking into account both the external environment and internal constraints in shaping and aligning organizational activities.

A strategic plan can be defined as a plan that integrates and organizes objectives and resources into a cohesive whole through intermediate goals and specific policies. Strategy helps "marshal and allocate an organization's resources into a unique and viable posture based on its relative internal competencies and shortcomings [and] anticipated changes in the environment" (Quinn, 1980, p. 7). Consciously planned strategy, rather than "muddling through," helps identify important issues and coordinate discussions in addressing those issues. It provides a general rationale for evaluating requests for additional personnel and financial assistance and for deployment of institutional resources. Good strategy can also help determine the desirability of trying to influence, rather than merely respond to, environmental change.

In formulating strategy, administrators and faculty must address fundamental questions of institutional activities in light of institutional objectives. For example, if they opt to retain strong core programs in all scholarly disciplines despite shifts in student demand toward professional and applied programs, then what strategies will ensure the continued strength and vitality of all the disciplines? One strategy might be to require students to complete a number of courses in disciplines which relate in part to their major interest and which would provide a foundation of general education for their specialized studies. Another strategy would guarantee disciplinary viability by taxing professional schools, such as law and medicine, that generate surplus income because of high student interest, donor attractiveness, or ability to increase fees, in order to subsidize essential arts and sciences.

Among strategies aimed at the institutional objective of remaining intellectually vital without relying on growth to add new faculty, one might be to increase faculty turnover by requiring departments to improve the age distribution of faculty over time and encourage early retirements in certain cases. Another would be to entice existing faculty members to retrain in midcareer in fields related to their own disciplines where more program opportunities exist. A third could be to encourage more visiting appointees, and a fourth might involve consortial arrangements with nearby institutions whose faculties have complementary academic skills or possibly a differing age distribution.

A noted Midwestern university recently conducted such a strategic review of its programs and objectives when it was faced with a serious financial crisis. Historically, this institution had provided a strong liberal arts and sciences program for undergraduates selected from a regional pool, but at the graduate level it served an academically elite group of students from a national and international pool. Increased enrollment could help alleviate the current financial shortages, and the university's reputation could attract students and the needed income. One option was to expand popular professional programs and continue emphasis on doctoral programs. However, placement opportunities in prestigious institutions were declining for the university's doctoral candidates. A critical review of institutional objectives led to a contrary strategy for maintaining quality: scaling down scholarly graduate programs and improving the university's financial position by increasing its number of undergraduates.

As institutions increase in size, complexity, and breadth of programs, divergence of objectives becomes the norm. Stated objectives in large institutions become more general, and some critics have concluded such generality reduces the usefulness of strategic planning as a management tool. But if the planning process leads from the review of objectives and the environment to setting broad strategies and intermediate goals, even general objectives can be definitive in guiding change. Establishing the weights to be given to multiple objectives occurs in the give-and-take of a political process, and administrators can help reconcile differing perspectives on future directions and bring to closure this process of setting objectives. Once objectives are decided on, administrators are also responsible for articulating them within and outside the institution and specifying them in detailed policies. If presidents and chancellors are unwilling to lead in developing strategies for implementing objectives, planning will not work.

Administrators translate strategies into practice through proposing and implementing policy. For example, teaching and research goals can be influenced by policies adopted for judging faculty performance. Policies on the number of graduate students admitted to programs affect research output. Policies concerning faculty consulting also influence the amount and type of research undertaken and the quality of teaching, as can those controlling allocation of space, support funds, and services.

Policies can affect student learning by encouraging their general education, facilitating part-time enrollment by relaxing course-load requirements, establishing minimum and maximum class sizes and teaching loads, providing academic credit for work-learn experiences, establishing off-campus learning centers and counseling centers, allowing students to take "planned educational leaves" to reduce attrition, and controlling student progress toward degree objectives with time constraints or financial incentives. Enrollment policy can influence the total number of students, their ethnic composition, economic distribution, distribution by sex, and distribution among academic fields.

Academic administrators can influence faculty hiring and advancement through policies on compensation and benefits and flexibility in allocation of faculty time. Successful administrators use the full latitude of options in academic personnel policy to assist in accomplishing a variety of institutional goals: developing hiring guidelines to meet affirmative action objectives, setting hiring levels above entry level for some positions to encourage recruitment of more mature faculty members to alter the age distribution, and splitting appointments between two departments to encourage interdepartmental cooperation. Many such policies require the approval of policy bodies within the faculty and sometimes of the governing board, but these legislative bodies are prone to rely on executive initiative to recommend changes in policy. Effective executives win approval of policies that support long-term objectives.

Establishing Planning Guidelines

Planning guidelines communicate institutional objectives, goals, strategies, and policies throughout the institution to guide planning at the operating level—colleges, departments, and service units. In business and industry, top management traditionally establishes guidelines and passes them downward to lower levels of the organization. In colleges and universities, an iterative process including faculty and administrators generates guidelines, which increases the validity of guidelines and broadens their acceptance.

Good planning guidelines have a number of common characteristics:

1. They provide clearly understood boundaries to focus the thinking of those who plan at all levels on desired accomplishments in the future.
2. They are easily identified with the objectives and goals they are designed to implement and consonant with strategies and policies.
3. The level of detail is appropriate to guide planning at various levels in the organization.

4. They are stated in a way that will allow responses in plans that are politically viable.
5. They are capable of being altered when the need is clear.
6. They relate to a specific time period rather than being open-ended.
7. They protect against unacceptable planning decisions at all levels in the organization.
8. They provide as much certainty for the next several years as possible, given the circumstances.

To illustrate, a university president may plan to reallocate faculty positions to balance workloads on his campus. He establishes as a planning guideline for one college reduction in faculty over a three- to five-year period by 5 percent. He may constrain planning further by disallowing any layoff of tenured faculty. This guideline meets the several criteria for good planning guidelines. Contrast this with the more common approach of calling for a specific number of positions to be released by the college in the next year with no reference to future actions that might be required.

Short-term financial, enrollment, and space guidelines are still the foundation of planning in many institutions for departments and other operating units. For instance, quantitative financial guidelines such as dollar support per faculty member or computer instruction dollars per student by discipline stretching, at most, two years into the future continue to be used extensively, with the result that departmental planning skips from the long-term general institutional objectives directly to short-term budget constraints, with a tenuous linkage at best. The intermediate period of two to five years, where major opportunities as well as serious challenges may abound, tends to be overlooked. Such tightly set and rigidly imposed financial guidelines also foreclose real innovation in planning and deter department chairs and other unit managers from including important unit goals in plans whose effects cannot easily be quantified (Quinn, 1980). Overemphasis on financial guidelines tends to favor less expensive programs, even when compelling academic arguments may exist for more expensive options. For example, a projected growth of undergraduate students in an economics program is likely to receive far less scrutiny than an equivalent growth in engineering if costs are the primary criterion.

Such financial, enrollment, and space guidelines are widely used because they are easily understood, are relatively easy to set, and are consistent with centralized planning and management. But other boundaries on planning, such as required annual rate of turnover of faculty, may be an equally or more important limit on the extent of institutional activity and in shaping planning decisions in the future. Such constraints need not be the only type of guideline for units as they plan. Policy goals such as lowering the time graduate students spend in completing degree requirements or increasing flexibility in current resources may also be guidelines for them. In fact, guidelines stated positively in the form of policy are likely to elicit more thoughtful and imaginative plans from operating units than is a list of finite planning constraints. Moreover, positive guidelines reinforce a more decentralized planning approach. One positive guideline would be to redefine budget categories to increase flexibility. This forces a reexamination of current expenditures at the college or department level in a less threatening manner than a planning directive that calls for critical analysis of current expenditures. Such an approach may generate efficiencies and innovations and will inform managers of real and artificial barriers to change.

Where specific financial, enrollment, workload, or other guidelines may be necessary, such as numbers of graduate students to be enrolled in a unit, "ranges" should be used both to allow for contingencies and to provide some margin for error in estimating, as well as to avoid the often negative reactions of units to tightly imposed constraints. Ranges may be impractical in cases such as space availability. Only so many square feet of laboratory space may be available for a given department in the short run. This is a fixed constraint. Guidelines can also be tailored to the distinctive needs of individual units in developing unit plans that match campus objectives. For example, a campuswide financial guideline asking all units to plan on the basis of a 5 percent reduction in staff and support would be counterproductive in implementing objectives and goals if agreement had been reached that strengthening certain programs, such as the biological sciences, was a planning priority.

Developing Program Plans for Academic, Administrative, and Support Units

Objectives and planning guidelines provide the framework for developing program plans of all operating units, including academic support units such as the library and computer center. Many approaches to producing these plans are possible, but all must reckon with the special structural characteristics of academic organizations: the intangible nature of outcomes, "shared" decision making, and the "open" nature of colleges and universities. Progress in planning at the unit level is best achieved by iterative dialogue between unit representatives and central administrators at all stages in the planning process. Such repeated exchange helps ensure that unit leaders understand the limitations and possibilities that exist in planning and that unit plans converge with institutional objectives.

This process of education, persuasion, and negotiation begins by communicating planning guidelines to each planning unit. (In a multicampus system, the parallel process of sharing institutionwide guidelines with the campuses takes place, but these guidelines are at a higher and more general level of aggregation than at the campus level.) Accompanying the guidelines should be an outline of what the unit is to include in its draft plan. Intensive, face-to-face exchange should then take place among the president, vice-presidents, deans, department chairs, and other unit managers until the draft planning statements are assembled. During this interaction, central administrators can help unit managers interpret the guidelines, react to tentative proposals, and come to agreement on unit objectives and plans. The unit managers' responsibility in this process is to advance their units as far as possible toward the institution's long-term objectives within the planning guidelines. This means setting directions and gaining agreement at various levels for change in programs over specific time intervals and then identifying strategies for achieving these changes, such as hiring one or more "stars" to round out program quality or encouraging retirements or resignations to increase turnover.

Many faculty members and some administrators question the efficacy of such an approach to planning, but the onslaught of financial shortages and slowed growth leaves open only centralized administrative fiat as an alternative to extensive faculty and administrative participation in deciding on plans and strategies. Unwillingness of faculty members and unit managers to engage in planning accounts at least in part for the ad hoc appearance of most reallocation decisions and explains why administrators often resort to taxing unit budgets as a means of reallocating resources. Plans provide a long-term context for resource reallocation: Planning discussions must be moved to the unit level, where many of these resource decisions have to be made, if these decisions are to be improved and if planning is to be a joint effort between faculty and administration.

Setting Multiyear Program Goals and
Implementing Resource Plans

Bridging the gap between planning and the traditional annual budget or resource allocation process requires an intermediate step of setting goals and resource plans for a two- to three-year period, where enough certainty exists to move the institution toward its long-term objectives. Effort spent in developing a process of this type has much higher potential for helping an institution deal with the challenges of the 1980s than equivalent time devoted to improving existing planning and budgeting practices.

This intermediate step shifts authority and responsibility over resource management from technical budget staff to academic administrators. It shifts the emphasis of resource management from dollars as such to the objectives that dollars should meet. It shifts the focus of resource management from preparing budgets and distributing annual increments of funds to achieving stable support levels and maintaining vitality and quality. And it abandons past practices of seeking accountability by detailed control over resource use in favor of achieving account-ability by allowing units flexibility in the use of funds and then assessing their performance and results in accomplishing objectives. It is not only a planning process, because plans require resources to become realized; and it is not only a resource management process, because without plans resources cannot be used most effectively. That is why Figure 2 shows this intermediate process as a halfway step between the planning and resource management phases of the management cycle.

This intermediate process lengthens the time perspective of unit managers beyond the current budget period by providing as much indication as feasible of both possible increments and decrements in future budgets. It creates additional certainty for their resource allocation decisions and is equally effective in facilitating and implementing program change whether resources are rising or declining. The process is at once both highly "political" and highly "technical," in the sense that it involves making decisions about academic program priorities on the basis of negotiation and compromise as well as good faculty judgment and technical administrative expertise.

This translation of planning objectives into multiyear planning goals and program and resource plans may be illustrated by the development of a school of administration at the University of California, Davis. A campus with initial strengths in both pure and applied sciences, Davis for some decades had as its long-term objective becoming a general university campus with a full array of graduate and professional schools. During the 1950s and 1960s enrollment growth and a supportive state legislature made it possible for Davis to accomplish virtually all its program goals except creating a graduate school of administration. This final unit in the long-term program had been approved by the regents of the university in the mid 1960s, but when the legislature failed to provide funding for the school, systemwide administrators postponed its development. Campus leaders continued to plan for the school, nonetheless, because it promised to add to the academic vitality of the campus and fill an increasingly important program need. In cooperation with the Riverside campus of the university, in the mid 1970s Davis opened a small pilot program in administration to test carefully the market for it and campuswide interest in it. On the basis of the outcome of this experiment, the decision was made to develop the school if resources could be found. Extensive analysis revealed that a school could be staffed and supported and a program of acceptable quality offered if internal reallocation was undertaken.

In cooperation with systemwide leaders, Davis administrators and key faculty members developed a multiyear plan for hiring new faculty, admitting students, and identifying sources of support and space. Anticipated retirements and other turnover of personnel on campus were projected to determine when positions could be made available for the new school. On the basis of this information, the systemwide administration then committed some forward funding from its resources to begin developing the school with the understanding that in time necessary faculty positions would be provided from vacancies expected elsewhere on campus and that no new state resources would be requested specifically to support the school. Necessary flexibility to spend these limited funds was delegated to the new dean, who used part of the funds for faculty and part for bringing consultants and advisers from other schools to help with program development, administrative support, and student and faculty recruitment. Professors in related disciplines were used extensively in this planning, and many are now serving as part-time faculty members in the new school.

As this case illustrates, strong administrative commitment to a campus planning objective, multiyear program and resource planning, extensive cooperation of faculty, resource flexibility and sharing among campus units, and positive incentives for the entire campus all contributed to the successful development of a new program despite limited funds. Such new programs can emerge from reallocation of current resources through careful planning and management of existing resources, if not with ease, at least with perseverance.

This example also points up the natural transition from setting objectives and establishing strategies to formulating multiyear program plans and implementing them through resource management. It illustrates the difficulty in drawing a clear line, if one is necessary at all, between planning and resource management, for in well-developed management systems their relation is indivisible. How resource management follows naturally from planning and blends with equal ease into assessing results will be the subject of Chapters Five through Nine, following further examples of dynamic planning in Chapter Four. From these examples, it should be clear why the planning phase of the management cycle is so essential. By setting objectives and strategies, by communicating them through planning guidelines, and by getting academic administrators and faculty to articulate more specific goals and how they propose to reach them in light of the resources likely to be available, academic leaders can use planning to make better use of resources in achieving goals and to assist in determining whether goals are being successfully met.

Establishing
a System for
Effective Planning

The experience of the University of California during the 1960s and 1970s illustrates developments in planning discussed in Chapters Two and Three, shows how a dynamic planning process can be implemented, and reveals some mistakes that other institutions can avoid along the way. The University of California is a large nine-campus public research university, with a longstanding tradition of shared governance and generous public support. Its experiences are applicable to individual campus planning, since interaction between systemwide and campus officers of the university is in many ways analogous to that between campus officers and deans, department heads, and other unit managers.

Stage One: Planning for Slower Growth

Plans for the university developed in the 1960s assumed that to accommodate projected enrollment growth through the

1970s and 1980s would require at least ten general campuses, each with enrollments of up to 25,000 or more. When changes in demographic forecasts occurred in the late 1960s, President Hitch appointed a blue-ribbon task force of administrators and faculty members to adjust enrollment projections downward as a guide to future planning. These new enrollment targets caused serious concern on several developing campuses whose growth would be arrested in mid-development and whose faculty had expected in time to develop in the image of the Berkeley and Los Angeles campuses. The president recognized that each campus would have to create its own identity and style. Gaining understanding of the need for a new approach to planning among campus officers and establishing a process by which this change could be fostered would take nearly three years.

In October 1971, President Hitch created an "Academic Planning and Program Review Board" to guide the development of planning in the university. He charged the board to (1) prepare a format and detailed guidelines for campus and system-wide academic plans, (2) coordinate the preparation of campus plans and supervise preparation of the systemwide plan, and (3) review campus plans in terms of potential redundancy and of resources required by various disciplines and professional fields.

The board was composed of six systemwide administrators, four faculty members appointed by the president on nomination from the chancellors, one graduate student, and two undergraduate students. It took them nearly a year and a half to develop planning guidelines and instructions for the preparation of campus plans. They asked campus chancellors to make a first approximation of projected enrollments by school, division, or college and by department or basic teaching unit over the next five years and to relate this tentative enrollment distribution to the objectives of their campus. (This five-year planning period was selected recognizing that the university makes commitments to students for four to five years and maximum commitments to nontenured faculty members for comparable periods.) Campus chancellors were also asked to submit lists of current instructional and research programs and projected additions to and deletions from this list as they related to future enrollment distributions.

The chancellors' responses were thoughtful; yet their lists of projected programs evidenced a continued commitment to further expansion. No chancellor wanted publicly to relinquish a possible claim on a new program even in the face of evidence that long-term need was not there, although in private discussions they all acknowledged that program additions would be slow to come. New evidence of willingness to share specialized programs across campus lines emerged, but most of this cooperation was the product of necessity and a certain amount of coercion from the president.

The most useful outcome of this first-phase effort was the opportunity for everyone to see for the first time the full academic scope and strength of the university, the present and potential areas of programmatic overlap, and the unbalanced development of some campuses. Since it was apparent that the sum of the parts certainly exceeded what could possibly be supported by the whole, the planning board decided to advance into a second phase that would emphasize planning to achieve quality in the face of constrained resources.

Stage Two: Planning for Financial Stringency

In this second stage, the board expected chancellors to reexamine their first-phase planning submissions in the light of resource constraints. Its record in developing planning guidelines for this phase was marked by minuses and pluses. Originally it asked each campus to develop program plans corresponding to its best estimate of resources likely to be available within the enrollment constraints that had guided initial planning and to explain how this estimate would change if more or less resources were available in the future.

Initially the president's senior staff worked as a group with the chancellors to orient them to a more realistic assessment of the future. Much was accomplished in "planning to plan," but the aspirations of individual campuses were strong, individual chancellors had to defend their campus priorities whenever specific programmatic disputes arose, and the president's staff was unable to spend the time required to work with all the chancellors. As a result, the staff recommended to the board a more centralized set of procedures to guide the chancellors' planning, and impose tighter enrollment and budget targets as constraints to planning. Estimated enrollments by graduate and undergraduate level were provided each campus for the current year and the fifth year in the future. Financial constraints were set at three levels initially: approximately the current level of funding per student, 10 percent lower, and 10 percent higher. Campuses were expected to identify how they would adjust to these resources in the future. Enrollment and financial levels for each of the campuses were made known to all. Administrators believed that this process would elicit a sense of priorities from each campus. Professional planners and technical staff at the systemwide level were interested in obtaining data for systemwide program and resource analysis, and they proposed extensive forms requesting detailed staffing, resource, and program data for each department so that plans could be translated into future "budgets."

This approach to imposing constraints was wrong, and it did not take long to hear so from the campuses. Campus staff argued that sufficient differences existed among campuses to render the proposed data inaccurate for comparisons among campuses and thus unsuited for systemwide decisions where every campus might be funded at the lowest resource level existing in the system for any given type of program. The chancellors rightly believed that planning guidelines needed to be tailored to unique campus needs, that these guidelines for each campus could best be developed through extensive discussion between them and the president's representatives, and that at least a part of these guidelines was best kept confidential within a small group of senior officers.

Despite initial mistakes, planning guidelines took shape and were endorsed even by those chancellors whose campuses were likely to be constrained in their future development. The rapport that developed between each chancellor and senior systemwide officers aided negotiations and interactions on other than planning issues. Chancellors were better informed about total university planning issues, while system officers were beginning to comprehend the intricacies and unique problems of each campus. The primary negative outcome was rising frustration among professional planning staff members at both the campus and systemwide levels, whose roles were beginning to change with the movement of planning decisions to higher administrative levels and who perceived that their influence in planning was being diminished. But staff frustration was outweighed by the benefits of the extended discussions between campus and system officers that pinpointed the need for intermediate-term planning to establish priorities among objectives for subsequent resource allocations. The discussions led to guidelines with a qualitative richness that made their necessary quantitative elements far more useful and informative.

Stage Three: Planning for Uncertainty

By 1975, after nearly four years of study and exchange between systemwide officers and the campuses, a new university plan emerged. It contained thirty-two separate planning guidelines to clarify and to make more specific the university's objectives and strategies as it faced an uncertain but different future. Even these guidelines, however, were inadequate to direct critical short-term choices as reflected in annual budgets because they stopped at the strategic planning level and did not lead to multiyear program goals and resource plans. Another three years would be required before this intermediate-term planning process would be developed.

Several statements of objectives and strategies drawn from this planning document, nonetheless, illustrate how even general objectives can be used to guide policy decisions. The primary objective of the university remained achievement and enhancement of quality: "Among the academic policy choices and planning decisions which the university must make from time to time, the overriding consideration will be insistence upon a high level of academic quality" (University of California, 1975a, p. 22). This general objective is based on the belief that the long-term academic interests of the university, the state, and the nation will be best served by preservation of high scholarly standards. The former strategy of building nine large comprehensive campuses to achieve quality was replaced, however. Three new multifaceted strategies for maintaining quality ushered in a new planning era: (1) "comprehensiveness and selective development," (2) "demand and balance," and (3) "flexibility and long-term commitments."

Comprehensiveness and Selective Development. This first strategy recognized that not all campuses could develop a full array of graduate and undergraduate programs. It specified three planning guidelines, among others, to assure quality by selective programming:

> Each general campus will provide undergraduate offerings in significant subfields of the humanities, physical sciences, biological sciences, social sciences, and fine arts [University of California, 1975a, p. 25].

> Certain undergraduate majors in areas outside the generally recognized core discipline areas will be offered on only one or a few campuses in keeping with levels of student interest and resource requirements [p. 26].

> In the area of graduate academic instruction, the university will enable each campus to develop selective programs which will avoid unwarranted duplication of those on other campuses and will contribute toward providing total universitywide coverage of significant academic fields [p. 27].

The first of these guidelines indicated the university's commitment to provide comprehensive undergraduate programs on each general campus, since undergraduates are not as highly mobile as graduate students, may enter with their academic objectives yet undetermined, and need an opportunity to explore broadly. Yet, the second guideline, that some high-cost, low-demand programs would be confined to given campuses, indicated that programs such as avian sciences, applied geophysics, esthetic studies, and biomathematics would be offered on one campus and not approved for others unless compelling arguments based on sustained student demand and low-resource requirements into the indefinite future could be demonstrated. The third statement advanced the concept of selective development in graduate programs. While guaranteeing each campus the presence of some graduate programs as a commitment to full university status and quality for all campuses, it indicated that future program decisions would be made in the context of meeting student needs in an academically and financially rational manner.

Balancing Demand and Programs. Several of the thirty-two planning statements were designed to address demand by students for programs, the need of society for scholarship, and the need of the university to balance the various disciplines on a complex campus. Two of these planning statements illustrate their thrust:

> The university will continue to respond to sustained student demand in appropriate academic fields by providing for adequate growth in those fields, although not necessarily on every campus. Current capacity may, however, set temporary enrollment limits in some programs [1975a, p. 31].

This statement indicated that student demands would not necessarily be fully accommodated as a matter of policy and that program balance, campus enrollment ceilings, and program capacity would be operative instead.

> The university's graduate programs, in the aggregate, will continue to be designed to fulfill broad intellectual and cultural needs of individuals and society as well as to provide preparation for careers to graduates of the programs. In connection with the latter objective, the university will seek to provide students with all available information about employment possibilities in their respective fields [p. 33].

This statement, with its emphasis on academic quality in graduate education, indicated that the university would continue to accept qualified graduate students into existing programs but would inform students fully of the employment prospects they would likely face. The alternative would have been to attempt to balance admissions with projected job markets field by field, a task considered neither achievable nor desirable by administrators and faculty. Because the university is a national and international institution at the graduate level, attempts to balance graduate enrollments in specific fields with state or even national requirements did not seem feasible.

Greater Flexibility. The plan acknowledged that long-term commitments of resources as a means of achieving quality, however desirable, had to be balanced against the need for greater flexibility in resources. New programs would need to be developed; new faculty members would be required to staff emerging fields; and resources for these programs would have to come partly, if not wholly, from internal sources:

> The office of the president and the campuses will develop further the existing policy of reserving appropriate portions of total available resources for temporary allocation according to need, in order to provide essential margins of short-term flexibility in the support of academic programs. This will be continued to the end that, whatever contingencies may arise, the university will be able to ensure the uninterrupted influx of new faculty talent, the development of new academic programs, and the maintenance of an appropriate balance of resources among and within the campuses [1975a, p. 37].

The implications of this general guideline were far-reaching. If academic programs were to be planned, instituted, and nurtured with resources drawn from lower-priority activities, procedures for reviewing programs must be available as a basis for setting priorities on program development, reduction, and disestablishment. Flexibility in academic and staff positions must be sufficient, and control of funds and information flow adequate, to assure that resources go where the goals and implementing plans say they should. If interunit resource transfers are made to balance resources against workload changes in a planned manner, acceptable techniques must be in place to guide timing, source, and destination of such transfers. If allocations of faculty and support are made on a short-term basis to meet the most urgent needs, means must be available to identify and account for resources allocated temporarily so they do not get "lost" after being allocated.

> Academic units should consider the optimum staffing mix of ladder faculty, postdoctoral scholars, and other temporary appointments in order to maintain flexibility while meeting total instructional requirements. Regardless of total staffing mix, ladder faculty will continue to have responsibilities for teaching both undergraduate and graduate students [p. 38].

This second guideline alerted the campuses to the need to increase flexibility in staffing through greater use of temporary appointments. Implicit in the statement, and explicit in the narrative of the planning document, was a challenge to review ladder staffing assigned to departments on the basis of workload induced by large enrollments in service courses. The statement affirmed the responsibility of the ladder faculty to teach both undergraduate and graduate students by indicating that temporary staff were not to be concentrated at the undergraduate level, depriving undergraduates of opportunity for contact with senior faculty members.

Approval and Implementation of the Plan

Systemwide administrators reviewed the planning document in detail with campus leaders, in part to improve it and, equally important, to broaden their understanding and gain their acceptance of it. Copies were distributed to campus libraries, faculty senate members, and student government offices to elicit comment and reaction. A special meeting of the regents was called to review the plan several weeks before they took formal action on it, both to increase their understanding of it and to allow for informal exchange among administrators, faculty members, and regents—including the newly elected governor. Even these efforts at communication proved inadequate, for it took more than six months after the regents approved the plan before any progress was made toward further refinement of its guidelines into program and resource plans. Completion of the individual campus plans required the next two years.

The campuses had been working on their own plans while the university planning document was being drafted. In several cases, chancellors developed clear planning objectives to guide decision making. At Berkeley, for example, Chancellor Bowker managed over a period of five years to build strong new programs despite some faculty opposition. The Berkeley planning statement commented that "redirecting academic efforts in directions appropriate to the educational conditions of the latter 1970s . . . is more a matter of marginal adjustment, through the evolutionary adaptation of existing programs, than of the creation of new academic units or new forms of academic organization" (University of California, 1975b, p. 3). Berkeley's new academic thrusts in natural resource studies, energy studies, experimental health sciences, law and society, and undergraduate public health, which more than marginally shifted its educational effort toward the technologies and professions, were developed, initiated, and nearly consummated by Chancellor Bowker before there was much public debate of the formal planning statement.

Planning on the Davis campus started with very general goals, but within four years new program thrusts included a rebirth of general education and attention to problems of energy, food, and natural resources. At San Diego, which had grown from a specialized scientific research institute to a general university campus, planning became a focal point for debate over its future size and academic breadth. San Diego lacked adequate social sciences and humanities programs, compared with other campuses, and strongly protested enrollment constraints imposed by the systemwide plan. This debate was not fully resolved in the campus planning process, although better understanding of the issues resulted from the process.

Given that these campus plans were the first in response to a marked change in the planning environment and the approach taken by the university as a whole, results were positive in beginning to guide policy and resource decisions. Nonetheless, the annual budget remained largely independent of planning and, to a degree, driven by external circumstances. Priorities were still set in the process of allocating what funds were actually received. Instead of planning "leading" budgets, the short-term nature of budgeting "captured" planning.

To try to tie plans to resource decisions, new mechanisms for resource management other than the annual budget processes were sought. Several possible approaches were explored with academic vice-chancellors, budget and planning officers, senate leaders, and a task force of faculty, administrators, and staff. After several starts and stops, the general consensus was that better decisions in both planning and resource management would result from ongoing, frequent, and direct discussions between campus and systemwide policy makers. Such a process, it was hoped, could replace the short-term focus of the annual budget process with a multiyear context for resource decisions.

After two years of trial and constant modification, a process for setting multiyear goals and implementing resource plans began to meet the objectives of (1) focusing resource decisions on long-term planning and policy issues; (2) agreeing on program goals, multiyear resource requirements, and problems; and (3) negotiating resource commitments to permit increased certainty for administrators at all levels.

Focusing Resource Decisions on Long-Term Planning and Policy Issues. A new management calendar provided a means of refocusing resource decisions on accomplishing planning objectives by restructuring management processes temporally so that planning preceded resource decisions. The calendars depicted in Tables 1 and 2 indicate how this was accomplished. Previously the main timetable for decisions was that shown in Table 1.

Table 1. Annual Acquisition Calendar for State-Funded Portion of the Annual Operating Budget (Fiscal Year Beginning July 1).

Month Activity Begins	Activity	Month Activity Ends	Period to Which Activity Pertains
July	Develop regents' budget	October	Year Y + 1
October	Review budget with governor's office	January	Year Y + 1
January	Prepare for legislative hearings	March	Year Y + 1
March	Present, defend, and negotiate state budget	June	Year Y + 1
June	Governor signs state-funded operating budget	June	Year Y + 1

Table 2. Multiyear Resource Planning and Management Calendar (Fiscal Year Beginning July 1).

Month Activity Begins	Activity	Month Activity Ends	Period to Which Activity Pertains
July	Administer current year's resources allocation	June	Year Y
	Develop regents' budget	October	Year Y + 1
	Review planning assumptions, estimate available income	September	Years Y + 1, Y + 2, Y + 3
September	Develop three-year planning goals and resource requirements	November	Years Y + 1, Y + 2, Y + 3
October	Analyze plans and set broad priorities in light of expected resource levels and resource needs	January	Years Y + 1, Y + 2, Y + 3
January	Negotiate resource commitments and planning targets	February	Years Y + 1, Y + 2, Y + 3
April	Distribute resources as agreed and modified in light of resource update	June	Years Y + 1, Y + 2, Y + 3

Table 2 indicates how discussions on plans, priorities, and resources were pushed further into the future.

Agreeing on Program Goals, Resource Requirements, and Problems. Next, the university's three vice-presidents responsible for academic policy and planning, resource management, and academic personnel made informal campus visits to meet with comparable campus personnel and learn more about specific campus program goals, policy problems, and the resources needed to meet these goals. Because these discussions were small and were conducted in a relaxed atmosphere on each campus, the need for political posturing greatly diminished, and systemwide and campus administrators could discuss problems and priorities in a context other than that of the current budget. As a result, what had often been thought to be resource issues turned out to be policy or management problems that had gone undetected or unresolved in past budget discussions.

Before these visits, the chancellors were provided with a set of questions related to campus academic planning such as the following:

1. The campus has stated that it intends, as a matter of high priority, to improve the quality of many of its academic programs. This will require new resources or rigorous reallocation of resources at the campus level. Thus, difficult priority decisions must be made in the next few years.

    a. We recognize that a substantial, legitimate need may exist to maintain and/or improve the quality of its core programs in the next few years to serve the needs of undergraduates. Certain programs may need to expand to attain "critical mass" and the desired level of quality. At the same time, there are doubts (from a systemwide perspective) about our ability or need to expand at the graduate level in most core fields. The question is how can quality improvements and some expansion be carried out in your core programs without unnecessary expansion in graduate programs?

    b. Professional programs, especially in engineering and administration, loom rather large in the campus's future plans. What steps will be taken to improve the quality of these programs? What is the minimal and optimal level of resources needed to carry out these plans? On what time scale?

2.　The enrollment plan calls for accelerated expansion at the undergraduate level over the next five years to serve the needs of regional students; then for substantial graduate enrollment increases. This plan assumes that resources will flow to the campus as a result of enrollment increases and that needed program development will be possible as a result. Under the circumstances, is this plan realistic?

　　a.　The freshman eligibility pool may have to be reduced to reinstitute the required percentage of graduating high school seniors as eligible for admission. This will probably be accomplished by raising admissions standards. If this is done, what is the likely impact on this campus? Over what period of time would the enrollment impact, if any, be felt?

　　b.　Given the possibility of severe constraints on further enrollment growth for the university as a whole and possible softness in informed student demand in many Ph.D. fields, are the plans for expansion of graduate programs realistic? Are they consistent with the goal of improved quality of graduate programs? Or will expansion possibly dilute the quality of existing programs?

　　c.　Enrollments in undergraduate, graduate, and professional programs are closely correlated to regional student demand. What impact will this have in looking to the future of the campus? Is there any reason to expect that this correlation will change in the next ten years?

3.　Assuming continued availability of new state resources, what additional resources will be needed to bring the campus to a desirable stage of programmatic development by the mid 1980s, when enrollment is expected to stabilize? In what sequence? Over how many years? Does the campus have greater need for academic support or faculty positions?

4. Recently the campus assumed responsibility for a large expansion in the health sciences program, including acquiring a hospital and developing outreach clinics. What impact has this had on the academic programs on the general campus? What impact may be anticipated in the next five years?

5. If the library needs to expand its core collection (as is asserted), what priority does the campus put on accomplishing this goal? If total campus resources must remain about the same, would the campus prefer to put more money into its library as a priority decision?

6. The campus is assuming that its faculty will grow and program needs can be met by new faculty positions. Because of fiscal constraints and the possibility of diminishing enrollment demand in the 1980s, most new faculty positions, however few, will be allocated temporarily. What provisions have been made, if any, to carry out academic staffing plans with temporary resources on your campus?

These questions directed the discussion toward planning issues rather than budgets—for instance, how certain financial, policy, or environmental changes would likely affect campus plans and how to resolve inconsistencies or lack of clarity in these plans.

After these meetings, the systemwide officers reviewed the issues raised during the discussion and placed them on the agendas of appropriate university groups for study and action. For example, during one round of discussions, five critical long-term planning issues were identified and put before the Academic Planning and Program Review Board. One was the problem of sagging faculty morale stemming from a variety of environmental factors, such as deteriorating laboratory facilities, rising costs of housing surrounding university campuses, and reduced opportunity to obtain outside research money. Another was the long-term impact that increased undergraduate interest in preprofessional programs was having on enrollments in humanities and social sciences and the resulting narrowness in too many undergraduate programs. As an illustration of the value of these face-to-face discussions, none of the chancellors had previously identified laboratory facilities as a priority for capital funds in the budget process, perhaps because they had little expectation that state funding could be obtained for renovation. Yet the importance to academic program quality and potentially high return from reasonably modest renovations led us to set improvement of laboratory facilities as a planning goal and as a high priority for nonstate as well as state funds. Similarly, faculty members and department chairs had sought to alert administrators that high-priced housing was (and is) a growing deterrent to the recruitment of quality faculty on several campuses. No effective mechanism had existed, however, to raise the problem as a major policy or resource issue with systemwide officers. Since it could not be dealt with adequately in the traditional process of developing annual budget requests, it had not received the attention it deserved until these discussions between senior campus and systemwide administrators.

Negotiating Multiyear Resource Commitments. Another set of meetings each year with the same participants was then devoted to negotiating a two- to three-year program plan consonant with both campus and system objectives. These discussions centered on how to translate long-term campus objectives into goals consistent with university aspirations and yet achievable within realistic resource levels. For instance, leaders on one campus believed that they could adequately round out existing programs with fewer than two dozen faculty members and limited funds for remodeling. This became the basis of a multiyear plan for the campus which would meet the university's primary planning objective of improving program quality. Resources needed to achieve the multiyear goals were determined and committed by systemwide officers. In fact, the number of additional faculty members agreed on by the administrators exceeded that which would have resulted from a traditional formula based simply on annual workload increases. All the new positions were committed for allocation over a two- to three-year period, in contrast to adding one or two faculty positions a year under an annual workload-determined budget process. This commitment meant that campus administrators could proceed with coordinated program development and with certainty about support.

In the spring, as noted in Table 2, senior systemwide administrators decided on specific funding levels based on best assessments of future income. "Best" includes careful assessment of both future levels and expected variation. Taking into account available resources and what would be needed to meet campus goals as defined in the site visits, they committed certain resources over a two- to three-year period to each campus. The final allocations and policy decisions of the president were then transmitted in writing to the chancellors. These letters provided a formal record of decisions on allocations, the permanence of commitments, any conditions placed on resource use, and how results were to be evaluated.

As a result, campus administrators and faculty members no longer believed that budget making was done in a "black box." Although technical staff who once had more influence on allocations now found themselves somewhat isolated from the budget-making process, their participation now came in other ways: They analyzed past expenditure patterns, helped project future income levels, and identified important environmental forces to be considered in the early stages of planning. Campus administrators, freed from trying to analyze what was politically the "best bet" in obtaining new resources and not having to defend resource requirements in terms of overly constrained formulas, could make the central administration more aware of the problems, opportunities, and resource needs of their campuses. For example, leaders of one campus had for years attempted to obtain increased funds for faculty support. The previous formula for providing dollars for faculty support services, based on a nine-campus average, had not recognized the specific needs of its faculty, weighted heavily toward the sciences because of its special program configuration. The faculty was so in need of support services that permanent faculty positions were being left unfilled so that these funds could be used to augment supporting services for existing faculty members. In the past, this problem had been perceived by systemwide staff as meaning that the campus had unused and thus "unnecessary" faculty positions, and on this basis the staff had argued against any further provisions for faculty. The new process easily identified the true problem. The campus was quickly provided with a "lump sum" allocation to help rectify current support shortfalls on the understanding that all its faculty positions would be filled.

In another case, overhead monies received for federal contracts and grants were allocated on a formula based in large part on campus population. One of the smaller campuses had consistently complained of inadequate research administration funds; yet the formula did not justify additional resources. The campus conducted a large extramurally funded research program relative to its size and, as a result of years of inadequate funding, had such insufficient staff to administer contract and grant funds that it had been threatened by the federal government for noncompliance with contract and grant procedures. The obvious answer was to allocate resources to reflect this level of research activity, but the formula-based allocation system was not designed to highlight exceptional needs.

The most exceptional case involved the Santa Cruz campus, which had a unique organizational structure involving dual faculty assignments to residential colleges as well as to departments or "boards of study." The university's existing budget systems could not account for nor display certain important information about Santa Cruz in a fashion comparable to other campuses, since unidimensional formulas could never capture its complexities. With the campus visit approach, the exceptions, qualifications, and complexities unique to Santa Cruz were clarified, largely through qualitative discussion based on informed judgments of senior administrators and faculty members. Quantitative data were used to inform this exchange between campus and system officers, but data were not the sole basis for decisions and instead served to highlight needs and guide decisions. The participants then became more open to persuasion and less inclined to argue over the data themselves. Staff analysis of data became more useful in decision making and its impact greater.

Summary

This seven-year saga of the transformation of planning at the University of California suggests that a planning process based on personal discussion among those who have leadership and advising responsibilities for planning and management at all levels more easily elicits good plans than impersonal, centralized, and staff-run systems. More ideas emerge, more conflicts surface for resolution, and understanding of issues expands. This process is far more satisfactory in a period of retrenchment than trying to set priorities by imposing tight constraints and expecting administrators to reveal publicly what changes they expect to make and the order in which they intend to do so.

The University of California experience demonstrates that formal aspects of planning, such as the existence of a planning board or committee, published documents, and letters of understanding, play an important role in providing a focus on long-term issues as well as a mechanism for communicating objectives, goals, priorities, and decisions. These aspects rid decisions of the ad hoc character that they take on when made in the framework of the annual budget process.

Communication at all stages of planning, while respecting necessary confidentiality, is the only means of minimizing charges that planning and resource management are "black box" operations. Without internal and, to a growing extent, external understanding of the reasons for planning decisions (as well as how they were reached), it becomes increasingly difficult to implement those decisions. Those most directly affected by decisions, either positively or adversely, must know about them before being informed by rumor or by the press. No better means exists than direct conversation followed immediately with written confirmation.

Although the iterative features of the planning process should be designed to accomplish information flow, evaluation, and reaction, consensus cannot be expected to emerge consistently. Therefore, the process must lead to a timely closure and decision on planning issues.

Finally, the university's experience also suggests that a decision to plan does not guarantee that good planning or, for that matter, any kind of useful planning will take place. A combination of education, leadership, management skills, and incentives is necessary to ensure quality planning. The major incentive is the knowledge that planning will affect future policy, practice, and resource use. To be effective, planning must result not in a plan but rather in directed change. And change can result only if planning decisions are fully integrated into the management cycle, including the management of resources and the assessment of results in light of these decisions.

Managing Resources
to Attain
Institutional Goals

Planning points the way to desired change, but academic leaders give life to plans by managing people, space, time, and money—the basic resources of any organization. As Jacques Barzun has said, "Administering a university has but one object: to distribute its resources to the best advantage" (1968, p. 95). Chief administrative officers can exert significant influence on the quality, size, number, and operation of all institutional programs, often through better planning and assessment, by improving communication and raising basic questions of purpose and mission, and by clarifying policies and procedures, but most directly by affecting the allocation of resources. Resource allocation is the most powerful management tool available to academic administrators. The constraining environment of the 1980s calls not only for better planning in higher education but also for technically sophisticated resource management in order to effect change in the absence of new resources.

77

"Resource management" encompasses more than acquiring resources and the traditional budgeting activities of assessing needs and allocating people, space, time, and money to them. It emphasizes anticipating likely resource levels, reallocating and "deallocating" resources, and finding ways to make better use of present resources through more sophisticated financial management, accounting, and performance assessment.

Today, resource management in higher education is inadequately integrated with planning and inadequately oriented toward making difficult choices among competing priorities in lieu of new resources. Many experienced academic administrators understand that to attain planning objectives requires careful and creative management of resources, but general uncertainty and threat of change complicate their adaptation of new resource management techniques to the decision processes and incentive systems characteristic of colleges and universities. In the meantime, challenges grow more ominous while opportunities to act are further constrained.

Resource Management During the Golden Age

During the 1950s and 1960s, the growth of college and university resources and the expansion of their relation with government forced greater administrative attention on resource management procedures, although these procedures did not necessarily result in improved management. Externally imposed budgeting techniques were not necessarily well adapted to academic institutions. Many newly hired professional budget staff were unfamiliar with academic management and did not understand how to work effectively with academic leaders in resource planning. At the same time, faculty members were asked to assume administrative posts for which they lacked experience, particularly in planning and managing resources. Together they implemented many management practices that now constrain the ability of institutions to adapt to a different environment and to manage resources effectively and efficiently.

For example, regarding human resources, decisions to hire faculty members were made independently of long-term costs; tenure commitments were made with inadequate regard for the age distribution of faculty members within departments and programs; and faculty members were employed to meet specific, immediate instructional needs with inadequate attention to individuals' capabilities to stimulate continued academic growth. Administrative and academic support staff were selected for immediate service needs without enough concern given to their ability to grow or attention to their development. High turnover among academic administrators encouraged bureaucratic regimens and large administrative staffs that became entrenched, making administrative change difficult. Inflexible administrative units were created to meet foreseeable needs, but when needs changed, they often remained in place while new units were added around them. Meanwhile, cumbersome and time-consuming consultation processes captured faculty time from more central scholarly responsibilities. In addition, state personnel procedures imposed special constraints on public institutions. State control over the number and grades of positions stifled incentive for effective internal management; state control of compensation rendered administrative use of financial rewards and penalties difficult; and the extension of civil service hiring, merit, and promotion systems to higher education staff personnel severely constrained internal personnel management. Now program change is constrained not only by these systems and by the narrowly specialized skills of faculty and staff but also by low turnover rates. Most faculty and administrators are less mobile now between institutions and within their careers than in past years, while inflation and changes in retirement laws are encouraging them to remain in full-time employment as long as possible.

Regarding financial resources, the time-worn budgeting practices of line-item allocations and precontrol of expenditures in many colleges and universities severely inhibit their creative use. Expenditures in specific categories such as travel, secretarial support, salaries, computers, and instructional equipment are predetermined even before allocations are received by the operating units. Approvals for transfers between categories must come from higher authorities, and because it is "politically unwise" for a unit to return unexpended balances at the end of the year, all funds will be spent within categories and resources will be used less than optimally. Although a department chairperson may determine by midyear that part of the department's budget for graduate student use of computers might be better employed as support for student field study, under line-item procedures this trade-off may seem unavailable. While small deviations in expenditures from budget are usually permitted under line-item budget allocations and precontrol of expenditures, reporting requirements and the fear of subsequent budget reductions can deter more timid administrators from taking advantage of the flexibility offered them.

In addition, administrative concentration on acquiring new resources, particularly in public institutions, has overshadowed efforts to improve internal analyses of resource needs and use. Departmental resource requests aggregated from the bottom up without planning and policy guidance tend to lock resources in place through political compromise rather than through agreement on goals first and resource needs second. As enrollment-driven formulas became the focal point for the external debate over funding levels for public institutions, internal allocation procedures were so strongly influenced by these external formulas that more internal formula budgeting was adopted than was called for even by funding agencies. And accounting for the expenditure of funds solely by fund source moved the emphasis of allocation away from the use of all available funds in an integrated manner to achieve objectives. As the number of fund sources grew, responsibility for fund management became fragmented, making coordinated use of resources to accomplish objectives difficult, despite careful planning and policy guidance.

Government practices constrained financial management of public institutions in a number of ways: Language added to appropriation bills to control expenditures became inhibitive. Withdrawing fund balances at the close of the fiscal year (a common approach to control and accountability) limited efficient use of funds by providing the incentive to spend balances to prevent their reversion. Legislative emphasis on net budget increments encouraged a sense of permanence in base budgets, while emphasis on annual increments rather than multiyear resource decisions deterred sound use of resources. Appropriating operating funds separately from capital funds and prohibiting trade-offs between them may have protected against serious overbuilding but it created an artificial barrier to efficient resource use and, in some cases, encouraged costly facility leasing and lease-purchase arrangements. Mandating programs without providing adequate funding to meet compliance costs also became a serious deterrent to good resource management. This practice has increased sharply as both the federal and state governments have sought to implement a number of policy objectives at little direct governmental cost. Compliance is obligatory and the objectives may be worthy, but requests from institutions for funds to implement the directives either go unanswered or elicit the suggestion that resources be reallocated internally to meet new "needs." And the desire of state government to control institutional expenditures of all financial resources, including student fees, private gifts, and federal grant and contract income, has restricted the efficient and effective management of all resources, has implied a lack of trust and confidence in college and university leadership, and has tended to deter many administrators from creative or bold resource management choices.

Regarding the management of space, institutions tended to build for specific "permanent" tenants and program needs, thereby limiting future flexibility. New approaches to teaching and changes in student interests have resulted in excesses in some specialized space and serious shortages in other types—for example, as the need for large instructional laboratory bays in engineering has given way to that for small spaces to house complex equipment, and as enrollment growth in biological sciences has increased demand for "wet" laboratories. Even physically compartmentalized administrative space has inhibited management approaches that rely on greater interaction among groups and individuals. The near absence of capital depreciation funds and renovation allowances in capital management programs has limited facilities renovation to accommodate these changing programs and needs. External constraints imposed by government agencies and local groups affecting expansion and space use include challenges from the surrounding community to further additions of space because of traffic, noise, or esthetic considerations; substantial government control over design and construction; and the dedication to austerity in design and furnishings that reduces flexibility and effectiveness in use of so many publicly funded structures for higher education.

Regarding time management, the tendency to segment time into separate annual budget periods has had a disruptive effect on the continuity of operations essential to good resource management. Faculty groups typically deliberate on important issues for extended periods, while administrators have been forced to act on these issues on short notice. Faculty bodies react slowly to administrative requests, often because they have not participated in planning discussions on the issues. Engaging faculty earlier in the planning process would have given administrators the timely and thoughtful support they needed as the planning horizons for higher education were affected by the shortening perspectives of external political processes. There is a need to lengthen the planning horizon, not shorten it, in colleges and universities; yet the political processes in the country are moving in the opposite direction. This is best evidenced in the lack of external appreciation for the longer time frame that academic institutions need for effective academic planning.

Stage One: Managing Resources for Slower Growth

During the 1970s, most colleges and universities saw real dollars decline, reduced or eliminated a few academic programs and faculty positions, and substantially modified their earlier academic planning objectives. Decisions were often painful, difficult, and unpopular; but some hard choices were made. Unfortunately, the initial responses to slower growth and strategies adopted utilized the resource management practices inherited from the 1950s and 1960s. They were short-term, reflecting a widespread attitude that the circumstances forcing adjustment were only transient. By their very nature, they often bore only a modest relation to a rational solution to long-term institutional problems and the attainment of long-term objectives. Priorities were set and decisions made in the absence of a planning strategy and often under crisis conditions. Without preparation for dealing with new challenges, these priorities and decisions further constrained options and foreclosed opportunities to meet them.

These responses took several forms.

Evasion. The initial reactions of some administrators were evasive—for example, understating the magnitude of the problem to themselves, the faculty, and the governing board; developing arguments to refute the evidence of potentially adverse trends, such as claiming that enrollment growth was inevitable because it was essential to the nation's continued economic development and prosperity; taking symbolic actions, such as forming study commissions and task forces to reconsider institutional missions; allowing expenditure of endowment corpus to pay current operating expenses; threatening to cut vital, popular, or highly visible programs, as by reducing library hours or health care services; developing a siege mentality ("circling the wagons"), partly to maintain *esprit de corps* and partly to buy time; and throwing difficult problems to higher levels of decision making, either within the institution or outside it to coordinating bodies or the state legislature. These palliatives failed to address basic problems, and some of them had long-term detrimental consequences. Tossing the problems to higher levels, for example, forfeited autonomy to these levels and set precedents for greater government coordination and control over future decisions.

Fund Raising. When these evasive tactics fell short, management effort turned to resource acquisition: increasing the fund-raising staff; undertaking annual fund drives; orchestrating external support for government aid; raising tuition and fees to offset increased costs; raising financial aid to keep pace with increased tuition and to maintain enrollment; making definitional changes in budget requests by such means as altering the method of counting students and redefining student workload standards, in order to maximize revenues; instituting user fees for public services previously offered without charge; and seeking all funds wherever possible for which the institution might be eligible—even at the risk of distorting institutional priorities and objectives.

Along with these fund-raising efforts, institutions sought to diversify their programs, clientele, and constituencies by instituting or expanding part-time and off-campus programs in order to broaden their base of enrollments. Besides recruiting more students, they sought to increase retention rates to avoid loss of revenue. These strategies were not necessarily cost-effective, however, in generating additional money. In some cases, enrollment increases actually resulted in a decline in available dollars per student. Some state legislatures provided no new resources for additional students, and some public universities saw appropriations decline at the margin as they enrolled more students. Administrators in both public and private institutions did not foresee the burdens that increased numbers of part-time students would place on student services, despite the significantly lower revenue they generated than did full-time students. And increased enrollments led to workload imbalances between departments, resulting in overcrowding and scheduling difficulties in some fields and pressing hard on academic standards.

Spending Discretionary Funds. The next step most institutions took in response to reduced growth and tighter budgets was committing discretionary funds, such as unspent salary monies, unrestricted gifts and endowments, and other reserves, to meet current operating needs. But this tactic created a serious loss in flexibility by reducing institutional ability to use uncommitted funds to shift direction. For example, one major state university in our survey group that suffered nearly a 50 percent cut in its organized research budget in one year replaced this loss with discretionary funds. By so doing, it was able to continue its research program for the next year at the previous level, but it lost indefinitely the use of a substantial portion of its uncommitted funds that had allowed it to gain distinction. In another case, a private university facing a large deficit forced academic departments to expend all their flexible funding to cover their operating costs, not only seriously sacrificing their flexibility and reducing incentive to raise additional funds but also merely postponing addressing the university's long-term financial plight.

Selective Cuts in Costs. A further step to reduce expenditures involved withdrawing subsidies from auxiliary enterprises, setting up internal recharge mechanisms, adopting full-cost accounting, reducing staff support, and cutting the cost (and often the quality) of supplies and services. For instance, recharging campus support services to academic departments became a widely used device as resources declined, although it also reduced financial flexibility. Recharging support services can, of course, increase efficiency in resource use provided the recharge rates accurately reflect the costs to users of the services they purchase. But if the recharge is merely a general tax to support an activity that has sustained a budget cut, its impact can be doubly negative—not only reducing the flexibility of academic units in their support budgets but also assuring continued funding for levels of support service that may exceed institutional needs.

Eliminating or reducing expenditures that could be deferred, such as building maintenance and repair, and equipment and library book purchases and replacement, was common in hopes of using funds for direct instruction. Most administrators now recognize that these "savings" from reduced maintenance and deferred purchases adversely affected instruction and research. Deferral was looked on as a temporary expedient, until resources could be regained to return expenditures to former levels; but this hope was not always fulfilled. Inflation greatly increased the cost of deferral; reduced routine maintenance such as exterior painting and waterproofing or upkeep of heating and cooling systems shortened the life of facilities and equipment, resulting in higher replacement costs; and deterioration in the quality of space and equipment impaired faculty and student productivity. Cutting support service staff was equally widespread and often equally counterproductive. In the absence of clear objectives or criteria, the tendency was to cut support services so deeply that faculty productivity suffered. In one university, services were so severely curtailed that the president was finally forced to provide emergency funds to restore minimum services.

Relying on Turnover in Personnel. Another tactic of cost reduction was to use "natural" attrition through death, resignations, and retirements to reduce the number of faculty and staff. Yet only by chance did vacancies match program needs. By withdrawing vacant positions from certain departments and reallocating them to others, administrators were able to counter some distortions in workload that were developing, but turnover was not adequate in many institutions to meet the personnel changes required to keep existing programs vital, let alone meet new program needs. Moreover, if institutions took positions away from departments where the vacancies resulted from adverse personnel evaluations or denial of tenure, departments sometimes responded with more lenient reviews in order to protect the number of their positions, thus inviting erosion of faculty quality over time. At the same time, a conscious policy of avoiding future tenure commitments gave some institutions a "revolving door" reputation toward nontenured personnel, hampering their ability, except for the most prestigious, to attract top-quality young scholars. And because most turnover tends to occur among younger faculty and staff, the strategy of relying on turnover tended to result in raising the average age of the faculty and narrowing its age distribution.

Cutting Costs Across the Board and Freezing Positions. Finally, nearly every institution imposed across-the-board cuts on the budgets of all units or instituted a general personnel freeze. Uniform budget cuts transferred decisions on reductions to the individual units of the institutions, but they were an expedient insensitive to differences in programs and the needs of students. Quality programs were treated the same as those that could benefit from extensive reorganization or even demise, and those that had managed effectively and efficiently received no reward over less well-administered units. General personnel freezes concentrated vacancies in the lowest-level support jobs where natural turnover is the greatest, thus requiring higher-salaried and overqualified employees to assume clerical and stenographic duties. They also tended to be particularly detrimental to small units, whose flexibility was already less simply because of their smallness. Like decisions to discourage any new program development, these cuts and freezes postponed serious planning and decisions based on careful assessments.

Stage Two: Managing Resources for Financial Stringency

Administrators who understood the long-term consequences of their initial responses to financial stress and who realized that their institution's financial woes were anything but transient looked for new resource management methods and policies to deal with continued austerity. Their "Stage Two" actions emphasized three strategies: (1) recovering flexibility, (2) reducing costs while increasing efficiency, and (3) maintaining program quality.

Recovering Flexibility. Rather than evading problems, administrators sought to recover flexibility first by educating faculty and trustees in depth about the nature and sources of financial and enrollment problems. Externally, they worked more closely with their professional associations in shaping legislation and government agency regulations. They sought to persuade state and federal officials to help maintain institutional budgets despite enrollment declines. They placed greater restrictions on accepting funds with too many strings attached; they assessed public attitudes about the institution through public opinion polls and contacts with community leaders and alumni; and they sought to improve institutional images through the mass media.

Rather than looking primarily to government for funds, administrators sought to raise more money from business, industry, and private sources. They endeavored to rebuild depleted financial reserves to help absorb the impact of future setbacks and capitalize on future opportunities. They designated some faculty positions as available only on a temporary basis, in order to reverse the trend of heavily tenured departments—recognizing that this tactic tends to establish two classes of faculty within academic departments and that the core of excellent academic programs cannot be built or maintained on temporary appointments.

Reducing Costs While Increasing Efficiency. In Stage Two,

institutional leaders began to phase out lesser-quality and lower-priority programs; reexamined their financial aid policies to reduce financial overexposure and concentrate aid more effectively; assessed institutional marketing, recruitment, and admissions efforts to assure greatest cost effectiveness; and made progress in holding down the costs of academic support services. For example, sharing of library resources among institutions and use of automated library systems became commonplace to improve service while reducing the cost of processing and accessing library materials. Outside contracting of some activities became an accepted practice, especially to avoid hiring year-round staff to meet seasonal or sporadic needs. "Off-loading" work from central administrative staff to departmental staff sought to reduce total costs. Students, after many years, were again hired to provide gardening, janitorial, and other services encouraged both by the nature of financial aid packaging and by lower cost. Across-the-board percentage budget cuts were replaced by redistributing taxes designed to distribute resources differentially among units over time.

Maintaining Quality. To assure the quality of programs, some long-ignored resource management methods reappeared that had once been commonly practiced in many institutions. Resource sharing within multicampus institutions and among neighboring institutions extended from the sharing of books, as mentioned earlier, to sharing of faculty, elaborate technical research equipment, and facilities. Most positive were serious analytical efforts to understand the future implications of present staff patterns and resource distribution, including analysis of present and projected faculty teaching loads, dollars spent for various purposes by various units, and the quality of performance of these units. These analyses provided the information from which reallocation plans could be developed and set the stage for current reforms in resource management.

Stage Three: Managing Resources for Uncertainty

Stage Three resource management rests on a number of critical operational concepts, among them the following:

1. Planning and resource management is a continuous process.
2. Any decision that commits resources is a policy decision. Thus, budgets are truly policy instruments.
3. Clear goals and assessment of results in light of them are better guides to resource use than detailed control over expenditures mandated at the time of allocation. They permit decentralized performance-oriented decisions rather than centralized tradition-oriented routine.
4. Flexibility in the use of resources can do as much as increased allocations to bring about desired program changes while improving efficient use of resources.
5. Assessing future fund needs, fund prospects, and constraints on fund use is essential for meeting short-term contingencies and assuring long-term financial strength. Such assessments permit central administrative officers to make commitments to units beyond one-year budget periods and before resources are actually realized.
6. Managing funds from a number of sources in concert can take advantage of differences in time of their availability and limits on their use in order to meet objectives more fully than managing and committing funds separately.
7. Face-to-face discussions between central administrative officers and unit managers at all levels, and among administrators and faculty, are essential for understanding of needs and priorities and for agreement on goals and resource decisions.

Resource management practices based on these modern concepts are available for use by chancellors and presidents in helping turn the challenges of the 1980s into opportunities.

Protecting and Enhancing Institutional Quality. To meet this first challenge of the eight described in Chapter One, academic program reviews by internal groups of faculty and staff and by external review teams can be employed. Among the factors they can consider in assessing quality are the characteristics of incoming students, national and international reputation of the faculty as judged by scholarly accomplishments, placement of graduates, ability of faculty to attract extramural funding, comparison of program characteristics with similar programs in the region or nation, and effectiveness and efficiency in using resources to achieve program goals.

Reducing the size and scope of one or more programs can also enhance institutional quality by freeing resources for reallocation to higher-priority programs. A more limited strategy is to require an adequate level of budgetary support before a department can fill a vacant faculty position. Special analyses can be conducted on resource use and relative levels of support among departments in related disciplines and among diverse programs. Understanding current programs in light of their use of resources is essential before resources can be allocated more effectively.

To stimulate professional growth, sabbatical leaves can be assured for those eligible; they can be focused on study and scholarship, with their objectives planned and agreed on in advance, and their achievement of these objectives reviewed on conclusion. Additional incentives that may stimulate growth include nonmonetary rewards for superior performance, such as citations, letters of commendation, and social gatherings to honor individuals. Outstanding teaching or research awards, grants from private funds to outstanding faculty members, and one-time bonuses reward quality performance monetarily without committing resources to higher salaries.

Junior faculty can be protected from time-consuming administrative assignments so that they have ample opportunity to become established scholars. Keeping senior faculty in contact with undergraduates and graduates in the classroom provides incentive for them to remain current in their fields and provides an important balance in approach and perspective for students. Disparities of workload brought about by differential growth rates among fields can be reduced by increasing flexibility in staffing through temporary appointments, such as lecturerships and visiting professorships. Where workloads are disparate, discouragement and low morale are evident among both the overworked and the underworked. Reducing inequities can improve the performance of both groups. Program and institutional quality are more easily enhanced when faculty and staff morale is high. One important contribution to good morale is an attractive physical environment. Dirty windows, leaking plumbing, and holes in the walls do not inspire the best from academicians, in spite of the reputation they may have for ignoring their surroundings.

Maintaining Financial Viability and Independence. To protect their resource base and acquire additional support—the second of the eight major challenges—institutions can emphasize development programs for diversification of funding sources; direct increasing attention to obtaining unrestricted gifts; scrutinize proffered gifts more carefully to determine what commitments of other funds will be required to meet their terms if they are inconsistent with planned program directions; and attempt to alter the terms of prior gifts and endowments carrying excessive restrictions that limit their usefulness.

Time devoted to improve management of funds already in hand may have as great a return as that spent in seeking new funds at the margin. Accounting capabilities can be improved to provide better information on resource use. Fund use accounting—the classical approach—may continue to meet fiduciary reporting requirements, but it is not particularly helpful for management. The more important information, from a management perspective, relates expenditures to programs whose outcomes can be compared with the estimated value of achieving goals and objectives or analyzed in terms of the least expensive means of accomplishing given outcomes.

Financial viability may depend on the institution's ability to adjust its expenditures downward rapidly. Inevitably, some programs will have to be curtailed to generate the revenues to pursue new academic directions. Program reviews are obviously necessary to these reduction policies. Transfer and layoff policies and plans to reduce or discontinue programs must be developed well before they need to be used in order to minimize the legal challenges that inevitably accompany attempts at reducing staff or faculty. Not to do so is poor management.

Although sound academic reasons such as tenure exist for much of the inflexibility in salary budgets, institutions can improve their financial responsiveness by employing more part-time, temporary, visiting, and other irregular-rank faculty. To do so requires careful monitoring of overall program quality, but the advantages in attracting people with new ideas and perspectives certainly warrant departure from traditional tenure-track hiring practices. Temporary or visitor positions need not be funded at low levels, as is often the practice. In fact, high salaries can be used effectively to attract distinguished visitors for shorter periods. In addition, employment periods can be matched to needs for services (for example, through nine- rather than eleven-month departmental staff appointments). Interinstitutional cooperation can share the cost of expensive teaching and support staff and facilities. Additional needed space can be leased rather than purchased by investing large sums of money in new construction, while facilities not currently in use can be leased to others.

Keeping Human and Physical Resources Vital. To induce program changes, deans and provosts can withhold faculty positions until potential appointees are identified who meet program specifications. Should opportunities arise to hire outstanding scholars to further these programs, funds can be made available in advance, in exchange for positions scheduled to be vacated through retirement in the near future.

Incentives to faculty members for developing programs and courses that further planning objectives can include personal advancement, added support for the program, "seed money" to institute a program, additional time to participate in the program, and removing constraints imposed on faculty members pursuing outside funding. For example, excessive internal rules on how extramural funds can be used need to be examined to see whether they serve the best interests of the campus.

To maintain vitality among faculty, administrative, and staff personnel, colleges and universities can expand in-service training and rotate job assignments. Variety in assignments helps retain interest and offsets some of the undesirable features of slow or no growth. Part- or full-time administrative duties can be assigned to some faculty members, not only for variety but also to make way for new blood in the faculty. Partial and phased retirement of less productive faculty members may be a desirable option for some. Generous severance pay and assistance in finding alternative employment are positive incentives to encourage less productive staff members to leave. In fairness to those faculty and staff who serve the institution well, it is essential that institutions encourage continued development and productivity in all employees and do all that is reasonable, fair, and legal to remove those who fail to perform satisfactorily for whatever reason.

Rather than creating new organizational structures with permanently assigned staff to handle possibly transient issues, administrators can assemble, on a temporary basis, necessary talents from different parts of the organization to deal with the issues. To revitalize a weak but important program, a core of faculty can be retained for a specified period during which the unit is strongly challenged to revitalize itself; otherwise the program can be closed down until the resources can be marshaled to reopen it with acceptable quality.

Needed program changes to maintain vitality are not automatic, nor will planning and resource management guarantee that necessary changes will be accomplished. Some business firms have experimented with "change agents" to encourage and inspire self-study in units and discover ways of strengthening, revitalizing, and redirecting current activities. In academic institutions, the closest parallel activity seems to be the accreditation process. Periodic self-study can be effective in stimulating program updating, but in combination with reports of accreditation teams and outside consultants needed change is likely to be more successfully induced.

Increasing Participation and Improving Access. Concern for improved access can go beyond earlier efforts to increase the number of students from underrepresented ethnic and economic groups. Admission requirements can be evaluated and broader criteria sought that will attract qualified students from a larger pool of capable prospects. Admissions personnel can adopt a strongly positive mode in dealing with potential students without engaging in unethical recruitment. Prospective students at the secondary school level can be assisted to meet college entrance requirements and to prepare for college and university study. Institutions that have adopted recruitment practices that are not commensurate with the academic values they espouse need to question the long-term benefits of stepped-up recruitment. Students should not be admitted who cannot successfully pursue the academic programs offered. Retention rates can be improved both by this policy and by increasing emphasis on faculty advising, peer advising, learning assistance, and planned educational leaves, or "stopouts."

Enhancing Operational Efficiency and Increasing Productivity. Allowing units to use all or part of any savings accruing from more efficient operations rather than withdrawing all savings to a higher level in the organization (as is commonly done) is a positive incentive for good management and a strong inducement to increasing efficiency and productivity. All academic departments and other units have a long list of worthy projects for the future. To be able to introduce one occasionally when necessary resources can be recaptured from current activities stimulates all members of the unit to look for ways of saving elsewhere.

Personnel policies that directly relate salary levels and titles to the number of persons supervised are a disincentive to efficient management and need to be changed. More sophisticated criteria should be developed that take into account relative responsibility, demands for leadership skills, sensitivity and centrality of the position, and the nature of decisions required.

Every vacancy that occurs in administrative and staff positions provides an opportunity to change the number of positions and management skills of the institution slightly. Such opportunities should not be left to chance, nor should automatic replacement based on present assignments be allowed without review of staffing plans. Equally important is the careful assessment of both short- and long-term staff requirements as they relate to new technology. Computerization, word processing, and communications technology are having profound effects on the numbers and array of staff talents required on campuses; yet many have been introduced without adequate attention to their impact, leading both to inefficient staffing and to extended periods of poor performance of service units after the new technology is introduced.

Assigning space to academic and administrative units to promote greater interaction and communication can contribute to greater efficiency in resource use. The quality and effectiveness of planning and resource management activities are greatly enhanced if those who must interact do not sense physical barriers to communication. Traditional "vice-presidential suites" and rows of individual staff offices are not conducive to modern decision and organizational planning concepts. Housing central administrative officers in different buildings almost precludes coordinated decision making on college campuses. In facilities poorly designed for interaction, both faculty and administrators must spend unnecessary time and energy in developing compensating—and usually more expensive—means of communication.

Improving External Understanding and Support. One immediate step all institutions can take to increase external understanding is to exercise more care in the quality of information that is made available to the public. For example, how faculty members make use of their time is not well understood off campus, nor is the amount of nonclassroom time that they devote to students and public service. Informing students, faculty, staff, parents, and friends about how the institution functions and the problems it faces can help increase public understanding, since these constituents are in positions to represent and promote the interests of the institution.

Public colleges and universities must come forth with convincing arguments to separate budget allocation levels from enrollments. One approach may be to focus the acquisition budget more on specific funding issues and program objectives that have qualitative as well as quantitative dimensions. This type of argument will be difficult to "sell" to budget analysts in state government but may be attractive to legislators and governors.

To preserve autonomy, it may be necessary to refuse government funds when the conditions attached to them become excessive, resist openly and often political intrusions in policy making, and, as a final recourse, seek relief through the courts. These strong measures may help gain a greater understanding among the public at large of the need to preserve a necessary degree of protection from political interference in higher education. Other changes in the way government deals with higher education could do much to improve efficiency in operations, although the chance of such changes is small. For one thing, allowing colleges and universities to retain part or all of any savings they generate and apply these savings to planned program changes would provide a strong positive incentive for efficiency. For another, a more rational basis for establishing accountability than through line-item budgets and excessive regulation would also improve efficiency. Accountability is absolutely necessary for any recipient of public funds, but current means of attaining it too often result in stultifying restrictions that stifle managerial ingenuity except in seeking to circumvent the worst of them. Another breakthrough that could greatly improve resource management would be for legislatures to adopt multiyear resource commitments as an instrument of institutional support. Legislators need to understand the time required to bring about necessary changes in program, particularly when appropriation cuts are considered. A fourth would be for state agencies to understand the importance of institutions' retaining independent control over nonappropriated funds and those obtained from government sources other than the state, if institutions are to succeed in developing private and federal sources further.

Learning to Live with Uncertainty. Steps can be taken to convey a sense of resource continuity in turbulent times and increase the ability of faculty, staff, and administrators to serve effectively when circumstances change unexpectedly. Increasing the potential mobility of individuals through retraining and job rotation is the most common approach in the business sector. Academic administrators can provide opportunities for faculty to increase their adaptability, knowing that persons with more skills and options are far more likely to retain confidence in the face of uncertainty.

Changing resource management practices can also help. Making advance commitment of positions and support to needy departments and other units, in some cases through reductions in other units, can provide a strong sense of certainty to units in need, while advance warning to the units losing resources enables them to prepare for cutbacks. Accurate and timely announcements of major decisions affecting available resources can do much to provide greater continuity. It is too much to expect good resource management among operating units when they can plan only from one budget appropriation to another with little information or guidance on what resources are likely to be available beyond the appropriation. Garnering of modest reserves to dampen variations in income over time can also reduce the impact of uncertainty and help achieve continuity.

Developing and Implementing Improved Management Processes. In a time of retrenchment, the procedures and criteria used in reaching resource decisions must be not only clear but reasonable if they are to withstand challenge. Those adversely affected may not like the decisions, but if they understand the process of consultation by which decisions are reached and the reasons behind them, debate can center on substance rather than on procedure. Periodic review and updating of all administrative processes can help avoid procedural challenges, keep organizations current, and achieve savings of effort and money. The traditional separation of academic, financial, business, plant, and executive management is no longer optimal. Administrative structures that bring together these different perspectives in an "open" decision process in which problems are collectively addressed, not defined and fragmented by functional boundaries, lend themselves to consultation and action among all administrative officers. This approach to problem solving and decision making should not be confused with an ambiguous organization in which the principals are unsure of their responsibilities or authority. The line is a fine one, but of paramount importance. Individual administrators retain their responsibility for action, but their actions are coordinated rather than unilateral. Rewarding those who function in this way can help make the normal mode of organizational behavior one of cooperation. Rotating administrative assignments can prepare individuals for this type of role both in attitude and in experience. "Matrix" organization may help facilitate interchange among administrative specialists if it avoids the tendency to become overformal and rigid. Faculty members with expertise in organizational theory, industrial psychology, operations research, policy analysis, or related fields can be asked for advice by their own institutions in areas in which their perspective can be helpful. Finally, for reasons more pragmatic than theoretical, more and more administrators may need to follow the advice of a number of astute presidents who maintain that the best way to encourage cooperation and coordination among units and staff members in achieving peak workload is to remain deliberately understaffed.

Already, chief executives on many campuses have adopted one or another of these "Stage Three" strategies for responding to the challenges of the 1980s with improved resource management. They are no longer preparing "for the past war." But beyond the eclectic adoption of discrete strategies, a consolidated approach to better resource management is possible. Chapter Six explains its elements, and Chapter Seven illustrates its application.

Integrating Resource
Management with the
Planning Process

Over the past two decades, college and university leaders have increasingly sought to base budget decisions on planning decisions. Yet the potential of linking multiyear planning and the annual budget cycle has not been realized as it should and can be. Figure 3 shows how new approaches to resource management can tie planning to budgeting. Based on the experience of the University of California and other major universities in adapting modern management practices to academic administration, multiyear resource management offers institutions increased flexibility, efficiency, and effectiveness in the use of resources. It gives managers at all operating levels increased authority and responsibility to decide how resources should best be used in meeting goals and provides greater certainty for these managers regarding available resources through longer-term perspectives on likely increments and decrements.

As noted in Chapters Three and Four, planning for a two-

Figure 3. Multiyear Resource Management.

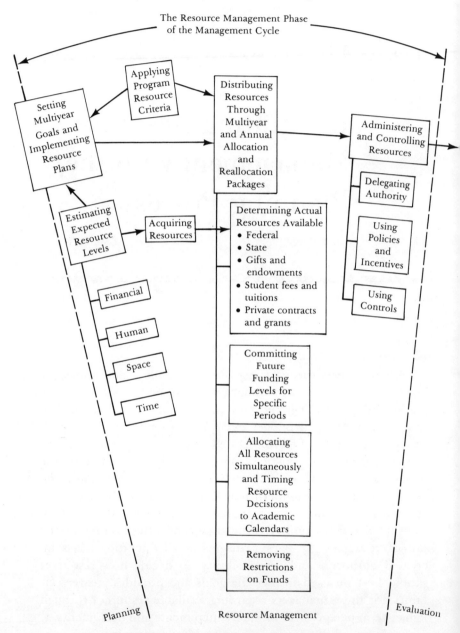

to three-year period provides both the opportunity to establish specific program goals that allow an institution to approach its long-term objectives incrementally and the needed sense of tangible momentum toward achieving these goals. Program goals are linked to resource use by a five-step process: (1) applying program resource criteria, (2) estimating expected resource levels —both of which serve as constraints on what can be accomplished over a given period of time, (3) acquiring resources, (4) distributing resources, and (5) administering and controlling resource use, all of which form the resource management phase of the management cycle.

Applying Program Resource Criteria

Program resource criteria are internal standards of the resources needed to support given activities. They are used, first, to assure that resources provided for a program are adequate to achieve an acceptable level of quality and, second, to identify resources currently assigned to programs that are possible candidates for reallocation. They can be expressed in such terms as student/faculty ratios, dollars of support per student credit hour, class size, or even the square feet of floor space to be served by a single custodian.

These criteria have some of the attributes of "budget standards" or "formula" but in several ways are more sophisticated in how they are prepared, used, and interpreted. First, they are program-specific in that they reflect the unique needs of given programs for resources. Undergraduate programs in physics have different needs than undergraduate programs in economics. Clinical psychology instruction requires different resources than does psychobiology.

Second, they are not single-valued, such as "fifteen students per faculty member" or "$20,000 support per faculty member." Instead, they are expressed in terms of upper and lower limits—twelve to eighteen students per faculty member, or $18,000 to $22,000 per faculty member. This flexibility accommodates short-term shifts in workload levels and allows for movement over time in activity levels before adding or subtracting resources. Use of such criteria provides a degree of certainty to unit operations and focuses administrative and faculty attention on goals, accomplishments, and real resource needs rather than adherence to budget formulas.

Third, criteria serve not as rigid requirements but as targets to guide allocation and reallocation over time in order to reflect new teaching methods, new research technology, and other changes. Serving as targets, they provide impetus to correct for historical biases in allocations.

Fourth, criteria are based on academic and professional judgments, rather than quantitative averages or central administrative staff theories. They have legitimacy for faculty and department chairs in discouraging creation of new programs or continuation of existing programs in their present form if resource levels are likely to be below the minimum threshold level indefinitely. At the opposite extreme, they provide evidence for withdrawing resources from well-established programs when these resources continually exceed those defined by the upper limit of the range.

As an illustration, many colleges and universities have established budget standards or formulas along the following lines: Junior and senior laboratory classes in biological sciences are not to exceed eighty students per lecture class and forty students per laboratory. If two laboratories are available that each contain twenty stations and two students can be assigned to each station, eighty students can be accommodated at any one time. The laboratories can be occupied six hours a day in two three-hour sections, five days a week. This level of use provides for adequate student access to microscopes and other equipment and allows for cleaning, restocking of student lockers, and laboratory maintenance. If each student attends two laboratory periods a week, the total capacity in courses using these laboratories is 400 students. If the institution has a policy that faculty members teaching at the junior and senior level are to average eight hours a week in the classroom, this translates into two one-hour lectures per week and supervision of two laboratory sections for a total of eight hours. Given these policies, five faculty members could meet the needs for these courses.

But because these standards are "point estimates," in that

they are fixed, for example, at eight hours a week with no allowance for variation, they fail to give much guidance to deans or provosts or academic senate budget committees when variation occurs. What if the number of students falls below the maximum capacity of 400? Are resources withdrawn if enrollment falls to 380, 350, 300, or 250? In addition, most resource management systems do not routinely monitor such standards for early identification of discrepancies. And in most institutions, space utilization, enrollments, and faculty time are each regarded as separate issues for analysis and action rather than as jointly used resources for offering a program.

In contrast, program resource criteria for these biological science courses might range between 90 and 100 percent in station use, allow for variation in lecture class size from 70 to 90, and permit variation in instructor classroom contact from seven to ten hours for upper-division instruction per week. With such criteria, the biology department chair, the dean, faculty senate committees, and other administrators can examine resource use, and the results can guide their future actions. Information on actual space use, the number of students enrolled, and faculty teaching hours gives rise to questions about future space needs and faculty needs as well as about the validity of the standards themselves. For example, if enrollment in these courses declines and remains below the bottom of the allowable range (350 students) for a period of time, staffing levels, support levels, and space assignments should be reassessed, particularly if other disciplines are increasing in enrollments.

Program resource criteria are best set jointly by those who allocate resources—senior academic administrators—and deans, departmental chairpersons, and faculty members who are responsible for using them to achieve institutional objectives, final authority resting with the chief executive. They should be reviewed periodically and independently of any particular budget cycle to ensure that they remain a sound guide for determining resource needs.

Estimating Expected Resource Levels

Where program resource criteria guide determination of needs, expected resource levels over the two- to three-year planning period set the constraints within which needs are met. Accurate estimates of likely resource levels are critical to making multiyear resource commitments, or "forward funding." They must be based on careful analysis of funds likely to be available from all sources—state and federal government, tuition, endowment income, gifts, unexpended balances, and interest—plus human and physical resources as well as existing commitments and legal constraints on how resources can be used. Presently, few chief executives or financial officers have a very firm idea of how much money their institutions are likely to have in the next two or three years, even from sources over which they have substantial control or influence. Income-estimating processes are becoming increasingly sophisticated and estimates more accurate, however; and because at least some fund sources are likely to be relatively stable over a two- to three-year period, it is possible to estimate at least the range of resources that can be counted on at various points in the future. Income analysis not only points the way to how resources can best be managed, it highlights possible levels of shortfall and where energies should be expended in augmenting income.

Because administrators have tended to view human resources, particularly faculty expertise, as largely fixed because of their own short-term perspective, they have paid less attention to anticipating likely changes in the distribution of academic and staff specializations than in financial resources. It has taken considerable time to recognize the importance of human resources as the prime instrument through which needed changes could be accomplished and to see as well the constraints those same human resources place on the rate and direction of change. But projections of faculty turnover and inventories of existing faculty and staff talents are now being carried out. When turnover is low, as at present, knowing what positions are likely to be vacated and what array of skills are likely to exist over the foreseeable future provides academic managers with vital information about how institutional goals can be met.

Determining expected space resources is less complex than estimating future financial or human resources because the buildings available and those being built, remodeled, or removed provide specific information for analysis. What is less clear is their condition of maintenance and their potential for alteration, which can affect future space assignments and use. Given present crowding on most campuses, accurate space analysis is essential to resolving the contentious questions accompanying nearly every space decision.

In determining resource levels, time is seldom considered as an element. Nonetheless, the distribution of faculty and staff time among competing activities is important in achieving change and increasing efficiency with few new financial resources. Faculty and staff strongly guard their independence about how they use their time, and surveys of faculty time allocations and changes in workload assignments are deeply resented. But if changes in the distribution of use of faculty and staff time are deemed desirable after careful consideration of both the short- and long-term implications of the changes, they can be best accomplished by educating faculty and staff about current and needed distributions and then altering incentives accordingly.

Acquiring Resources

Resource acquisition includes all activities related to marshaling the financial, human, space, and time resources required to implement plans and strategies. Because funds come from a wide variety of sources, this is one of the most diverse and complicated management activities. Responsibilities for resource acquisition are typically fragmented and inadequately coordinated; budget officers, endowment officers, financial aid officers, and contract and grant officers and recipients all acquire and expend resources.

As resources have tightened, increasing effort has gone into their acquisition. Private institutions have focused their fund-raising activities largely on attracting additional gift money and federal money while seeking better internal management of what resources they have. Public institutions have emphasized improving their ability to convince the state that the current budget base must be honored, that more money is needed to keep pace with inflation, and that any new activities require additional appropriations. Professional budget staff have worked hard on mastering the "external budget game," often at the expense of improving the management of current resources. External schedules and external priorities thus tend to dominate internal management, with resource acquisition becoming the pivot around which all other management activities turn. Because the political decision calendar runs from fiscal year to fiscal year, institutions have geared both their external acquisition and internal allocation to this calendar whether or not it meets fully the internal management needs.

Multiyear resource management can assist in better articulating resource priorities and may increase success in resource acquisition by guiding and influencing what resources are sought, from whom they are sought, and what constraints on funds are acceptable. Further, because it separates external acquisition from internal allocation, it helps break the lock step between external budgetary appropriations and internal allocations. With a planning calendar such as that outlined in Chapter Four, annual acquisition can be conducted almost independently of the allocation process.

To succeed at resource acquisition requires direction and coordination by the chief executive with the assistance of the principal financial officer; and all those responsible for acquiring resources must have a clear idea of expected needs. Targeted and tightly argued budget requests are more successful than weakly developed ones, and budget requests reflecting careful planning and resource management are easier to document, present, and defend. They place an institution in a position to state clearly and strongly its own internal objectives, priorities, and resource needs.

Such a planned approach to resource acquisition provides a strong counter to external forces that sometimes exert too much influence on staff in the budget development and defense process as well as in internal resource decisions by distorting institutional priorities. It offers a means by which colleges and universities can be appropriately accountable for the expenditure of public monies, since they cannot expect less external control over expenditures without demonstrating the efficient achievement of generally agreed-on goals.

Public colleges and universities, being heavily dependent on state appropriations, are aware of the many opportunities governmental bodies have to influence internal program decisions and priorities by exercising control over the budget and its expenditures. As resources have become more limited, these opportunities have grown. Yet few examples exist of public institutions refusing to take public money because of excessive control over its use. In contrast, many private colleges and universities are acutely sensitive to the potential for governmental intrusion as their dependence on public support increases. They have not only argued forcefully to retain control over internal operating decisions, particularly about issues related to hiring practices and financial reporting requirements, but in some cases have refused public funds because of such constraints.

Though difficult to achieve, new bases to replace past growth-oriented formulas can be sought on which to establish levels of public support. Whether "block budgeting" or some other form of allocation, new bases are in the best interests of both colleges and universities and government. There is as little justification for budget cutting solely on demographic trends or declining enrollments as there is for defending the sanctity of base budgets and of continued upward adjustments in them to offset the full effects of inflation. Negotiating improved allocation bases will be difficult at best, calling for statesmanship on all sides. Colleges must demonstrate the ability to be accountable for their resource expenditures. Government must be convinced that college and university programs are too important to be reshaped by short-term political choices or changes in direction.

Distributing Resources

Allocating resources to operating units to help achieve multiyear goals sets the resource management activity in motion. Department chairs and other unit managers gain certainty in working toward these goals when central administrators improve resource distribution in several specific ways—by committing resources for specific periods of time in the future, giving advance notice of decrements as well as increments in resources, allocating at one time all funds a unit will receive in a given budget period, and reducing the effect of restrictions on fund use.

These techniques contrast with those of the growth period as well as most present practices. During growth, units considered every budget increase they received to be permanent, since allocations obviously could only go up, not down. When resources tightened and administrators wanted to create "flexibility," they began allocating and deallocating funds on a "temporary" one-year basis, which shortened units' planning horizons and increased their operating uncertainty. Once units became unsure of what resource levels they could expect, or indeed what the "rules" for allocating funds were, they tended to make less than optimal decisions that in some cases compromised program quality—filling vacant faculty positions with "available" candidates because of fear the positions might be lost if left unfilled too long; continuing to recruit and admit more students while expecting that more funds would be made available once it became clear to central administrators that workloads had increased; and secreting funds coming from outside sources, knowing that any appearance of affluence would mean that other funds would likely be withheld.

Committing Future Funding Levels for Specific Periods. Any management practices that add certainty to decision making, even if only the certainty that resource levels will be lower than at present, tend to improve the quality of these decisions. Multiyear allocations as discussed in Chapters Three and Four can add certainty. Units can plan more effectively if administrators can convey with some confidence likely future resource levels so that department chairs and faculty members or the managers of other units can expect a certain percentage addition or deletion at specific times in the next several years (even if the resources will not be available for two or three years). Commitment to making necessary adjustments in activities and staffing to accomplish program goals will be strengthened.

Committing future resource levels requires determining what funds are now available and are likely to be available over the next few years and then negotiating resource levels for given periods in light of long-term objectives, intermediate planning goals, program resource criteria, and these estimates of future resources. For example, if administrators foresee no way of avoiding enrollment decline and a consequent reduction in tuition income within five years, all the income from tuition over the intervening four years might not be used during each of those years, and commitments of funds from this source could be systematically curtailed in the interim.

Various degrees of certainty can be attached to these commitments. "Committed" funds are those that the administration agrees to provide without qualification over the period. Marginally allocated, or "targeted," funds carry less certainty. It is management's job to avoid making commitments without adequate assurance of available resources, while assuring the availability of resources in order to make these commitments as far ahead as possible. For instance, central administrators may decide that it is prudent to firmly commit only 80 percent of total institutional funds expected in the next year and 70 percent of those expected in the third year. This commitment requires that internal reserves or external funds be sufficient to guarantee each unit the amount of money promised to it even if revenue shortfalls occur. Beyond these "committed" funds, another 10 or 15 percent can be "targeted" for allocation, based on the best possible assessment of funds likely to be available beyond the multiyear period, even though they are not guaranteed. With a rolling multiyear planning and resource allocation process, allocations constantly progress from "soft" targets to firm commitments as the years pass. Units know that to become commitments, intermediate-period targets depend on planned income levels being reached. This approach to future funding maintains the flexibility currently achieved by distinguishing between "permanent" and "temporary" allocations. It also diminishes uncertainty by providing advance notice of intended increases and advance warning of pending reductions in resources. It further allows administrators to efface the now sharp distinction between base budgets and annual increments, thus removing one more barrier to redirection and reallocation.

Allocating All Resources Simultaneously and Timing Decisions to Academic Calendars. A second practice to provide greater certainty and make more effective use of resources is, insofar as possible, to allocate at one time all funds a unit can expect to receive during the year. When this is not done, unit managers are hampered in making choices all through the budget period. They may avoid commitments early for fear of being unable to meet subsequent needs and either end the period with unexpended resources or else spend balances less thoughtfully at the end of the period.

Administrators must develop mechanisms to compensate for the fact that resource allocations by external agencies are not matched to the demands of the academic year. Fiscal and academic calendars seldom run concurrently, particularly in public universities, giving rise to uncertainty about resources during the academic year. For instance, when the amount of forthcoming federal or state student financial aid money is not known at the time admission decisions are made, caution typically prevails, so that when funds are released, it is often too late to attract qualified students, and the funds frequently go unspent.

Removing Restrictions on Funds. Reducing fund identification can improve fund use still further. Most institutions tend to manage funds by source, and unless externally imposed constraints on the use of these funds that limit their effectiveness can be changed, these constraints must, of course, be honored. Earmarked monies can move organizations in desired directions, but they are known to be inefficient. For example, funds called "equipment replacement" monies provide incentives for departments to develop "needs" for equipment because the money is available. Funds earmarked for capital improvements may better be used to meet pressing needs for improved plant maintenance. Agreement on goals, objectives, and supporting policy as well as economic incentives is needed in order to reduce or eliminate such earmarking or precontrolling by fund source. Changes in governing board or presidential authority over institutionally controlled funds may also be necessary, along with changing legal restrictions on gifts and bequests and convincing external funders of the merit of greater flexibility in how their funds can be used.

Administering and Controlling Resource Use

Currently, planning and operating decisions are tending toward greater centralization in higher education—a nearly universal symptom of organizational stress. Faculty authority over academic planning, salary, and program decisions is being subtly reduced and assumed by administrators. Administrative and academic support services are being consolidated in the interests of efficiency, with the consequence that top administrators increasingly involve themselves in operating details. And department chairs have been forced to relinquish some of their former authority to higher levels. Increasing uncertainty and turbulence will likely exacerbate these trends in the future. Yet centralization is antithetical to good academic management, as illustrated by the recent questionable planning and resource management decisions described in Chapters Two and Five.

The critical decisions needed during uncertainty, such as setting priorities for resource use within programs and between programs, determining when curricula need to be renovated or dismantled, and planning the most effective array of faculty talents, cannot be established effectively from on high. Rather than "Do this and that," the operating principle must be "Do whatever is necessary to achieve agreed-on objectives effectively and efficiently." This management principle provides extensive freedom for department chairs and other managers to act relatively independently within plans, policies, and delegations of authority.

Proponents of centralized authority argue that, in the absence of central control, excessive time is taken to gain acceptance of, and implement, changes in an organization. But in academic organizations, no significant change in academic activities is likely without the support or at least the neutrality of the faculty. Faculty opinions are shaped and action encouraged more effectively through education than by directives from a central administrative office. Decentralization of operating decisions provides the key to successful academic management. Decentralization requires that administrators educate the faculty about the future, that some planning for the future has taken place, and that the means of assessment are operational. Such education is necesssary if resource administration is to be decentralized to departments. Reliance on precontrol of units through detailed resource allocations and expenditure constraints expressed through a multitude of rules and procedures can be replaced with a modern resource management approach relying on delegated authority, policy guidance, economic incentives, and assessment of results. Only those central controls needed for fiduciary responsibility and effective coordination should be retained.

Responsibility and authority can be delegated from governing boards through central administrators to operating levels, where information about programs is the greatest. The choices most clearly in evidence at the operating level can be used to define the scope of decisions and operational authority, encourage managerial action to the limit of the delegation, and serve as a frame of reference in evaluating managerial personnel performance. Delegations and redelegations of authority essential to a decentralized mode of operation require (1) coordination to achieve consistency and compatibility and (2) attention to means of inducing required consultation in keeping with shared governance.

Policy statements provide the framework within which operating decisions are made. For example, adoption of a policy of offering small classes to freshmen and sophomores may require department chairs and faculty committes to reassign faculty members to courses and reallocate funds to instructional resources from upper-division and graduate levels and from research. Similarly, policies as diverse as affirmative action hiring goals, payment for overtime by staff members, use of space, teaching workloads, and support required before a position can be filled circumscribe individual decisions.

The effect of such policies on resource use and goal attainment is generally underestimated. In a decentralized approach, policies to achieve given results take on great importance because operating decisions are left to lower levels in the organization and policies are relied on heavily to guide those decisions.

More careful review of policies is required to ensure that they aid the implementation of objectives and that unforeseen negative side effects are minimized.

Colleges and universities have had long experience in shaping faculty behavior by rewarding superior teaching, research, and other creative and service activities with advancement in rank, salary, and public recognition. But the use of policies as incentives, both positive and negative, to accomplish planning objectives is underdeveloped; rules and procedures are overly relied on for dictating resource use. Policies that provide positive incentives include allowing units to retain, rather than withdrawing, all or part of the resources they can generate through improved operating efficiency in meeting program objectives; advancing funding to a department for an exceptional planned change, allowing the department to repay over time as it generates the resources; providing matching funds to any unit that agrees to implement a desired program change; and rewarding good academic administrators not only with personal recognition such as salary increases but with additional financial encouragement for their unit.

Negative incentives that provide penalties for imprudent choices include cutting the budgets of units that manage poorly or fail to achieve objectives, while providing additional resources for needy or well-managed units; providing little or no salary recognition to less able administrators until performance improves; or removing some delegated authority from such administrators and transferring it to higher levels.

Some controls are obviously necessary not only to meet fiduciary responsibility but to provide information to adjust expenditures during the operating period. Because resource expenditures must be used to accomplish specific goals, it is prudent to examine periodically how funds are being spent and are likely to be expended relative to these goals. Present fiduciary controls such as accounting rules may specify the purposes of expenditures, but they are more often procedural, specifying how and when expenditures are to be reported. Auditing as a control ensures that proper procedures are followed and that resources are directed toward predetermined ends. Another type of control is available to assemble information on which sequential corrective decisions can be based in the course of a budget period. This type, known as "feedforward" control (Koontz and Bradspies, 1972), is illustrated informally by staff as they examine planned expenditures, project these expenditures forward, and correct spending plans for the remainder of the budget period. Effective feedforward control in a decentralized management system requires timely information properly distributed. For example, a department may have established a goal of providing funds for faculty travel sufficient to allow each faculty member to attend one national professional meeting a year, provided his or her research paper is accepted for presentation. The budgeted amount is based on recent experience of one quarter of the faculty having papers accepted in any one year. Three months into the budget period, feedforward control may provide information that over one quarter of the faculty have been invited to present their research. Administrators, with faculty counsel, can then decide whether to fund only those first accepted, partly fund all, or plan internal budget reallocations within allotted funds to meet the goal fully, even at the expense of other unit goals. Such information can also indicate whether it will be possible to take advantage of new opportunities to achieve goals, but administrators must have authority to shift resources.

Conclusion

Multiyear planning and resource management clearly entails substantial changes in "budgeting" as conventionally practiced. It stretches out the time frame for resource decisions; it separates the acquisition of resources from internal resource management; it moves from earmarking monies for specific purposes to "packaging" resources from many sources to meet agreed-on program objectives; it calls for coordinated resource decisions, in terms of both substance and timing; and it calls for achieving greater flexibility in how funds can be used, and shifts the focus from controlling fund use to providing greater latitude to unit managers for decisions with after-the-fact review of performance.

In addition, it calls for faculty and administrative cooperation in planning and resource decisions. Administrators need
to recognize the role of faculty members in providing knowledge and judgment on resource issues, to confide more directly
with them on emerging problems, and to seek their advice
through regular channels before crises develop. At the same
time, faculty members who serve in advisory roles must broaden
their perspectives regarding the campus and its well-being, work
to improve the information on which their judgments are based,
maintain absolute objectivity, and insist on documentable quality analysis from themselves and their colleagues.

The potential pitfalls are numerous. Faculty members
easily succumb to the temptation to second-guess administrative
decisions after the fact rather than concentrate on improving
their contribution to decisions before they are made. Many faculty members retain a constituency attitude of representing
their disciplinary colleagues when called on to serve the greater
campus. And they have a penchant for overorganizing to meet
their responsibilities in planning and resource management rather than concentrating their effort in a small but effective core
committee and engaging other assistance on an ad hoc, short-
term basis as specific needs arise. Overorganization gives rise to
procedural and jurisdictional conflicts and delayed responses,
two outcomes that can quickly negate the usefulness of faculty
participation in planning and resource management.

For faculty members to serve effectively on planning and
resource management committees, time is required to "learn the
ropes" and to establish the necessary working relationships with
one another and with administrators. Three-year appointments
should be considered a minimum, and the members should be
prepared to commit long hours each week in the intensive study
and discussion that such service entails.

Despite these difficulties, multiyear resource management
offers increasing potential to colleges and universities during the
rest of the 1980s—among other reasons, because of its utility in
the management of retrenchment. One example involves a state
university that experienced a sharp decline in enrollment during
the early 1970s. As so often when enrollment drops, some essential programs were still developing and required additional

resources to achieve an acceptable level of quality. Yet on the basis of workload statistics, not even the present number of faculty members and funding could be justified. The university could relinquish a few positions immediately, but to absorb the entire cut within a year would have meant not reappointing some of the new and most valuable academic staff.

A multiyear resource plan was devised for the campus that accomplished several gains: (1) it provided time for the administration to educate the campus community about the gravity of the situation, (2) it put departments on notice that, in the absence of enrollment recovery, an additional number of positions would be withdrawn over a specified period, (3) it allowed them to review their academic programs to determine where further cuts could be made that would free resources consistent with plans, (4) it minimized confusion and loss of faculty morale, which would have likely discouraged some potential students from enrolling and encouraged some of the most-needed faculty members to depart, (5) it provided time to assist faculty members in overstaffed areas to be retrained or to find positions in other institutions, (6) it bought time for departments to work with one another and with neighboring institutions in developing cooperative programs that shared limited resources and attracted new students, (7) it stimulated more systematic efforts at student recruitment and retention and at diversified fund raising, and (8) perhaps most important, it demonstrated to state officials enough foresight and effort that they were willing to help the campus work through the period of retrenchment without repressive restrictions.

The political dimensions of resolving an issue of this magnitude through improved resource management were significant. As resources had shrunk, pressures had mounted for quick and drastic action. Some legislators as well as some faculty and administrators had pressed for laying off nontenured faculty immediately. Others had seized the opportunity to challenge the entire concept of tenure. A multiyear approach to resource management did not eliminate these political pressures, but it allowed institutional leaders to challenge the most extreme of them by demonstrating that a systematic and methodical effort at retrenchment could avoid disaster.

In another large public university in the Midwest, enrollment dropped nearly one-third in the first half of the 1970s, largely as a result of a change in state policy toward funding out-of-state students. The budget was severely out of balance even though ameliorative steps to reduce expenses and increase income had been taken. The president created an administrative-faculty-student advisory council to recommend funding priorities to him; he asked deans to reduce base budgets over a three-year period; and he devised a multiyear resource management plan. This represented an unprecedented action of sharing facts that previously had been known only by senior administrators. The really innovative action was placing the difficult questions of funding priorities before an administrative-faculty-student group.

Two interesting repercussions of this planning mode emerged: Faculty interest in collective bargaining has lessened now that the faculty senses its improved role in institutional planning and resource management. And the ability of the university to grapple successfully with retrenchment impressed private funders to the extent that private endowment has risen sharply over the past five years.

This university faces stiff challenges ahead because of further expected enrollment declines, but its faculty and administrators alike seem to have evolved a joint approach that is resolving present problems and is promising continued improvements in resource management and resolution of future challenges.

7

Implementing
New Resource
Management Concepts

To illustrate the application of the elements and principles of resource management presented in Chapter Six, this chapter describes nearly a decade of effort to improve systemwide resource management in the University of California. It shows what can be done to improve resource management practices as well as mistakes to avoid in changing longstanding fiscal and budgeting practices. Although there are differences in how institutions are funded and the degree of control administrators can exercise over resources, the University of California experience should nevertheless prove helpful.

Stage One: Resource Management During Slower Growth

When growth was the primary challenge during the 1950s and 1960s, the University of California, like most other public colleges and universities, adopted formulas that related resource

needs and workload criteria to enrollment levels, both for pre-
senting budget needs to the governor and legislature and for
justifying internal allocations. As growth continued into the
1960s, these budget formulas became more detailed and sophisticated. In the late 1960s, however, the state began to challenge
these formulas, partly because of its own assessment of future
growth and partly because of dissatisfaction with internal resource management.

When the university began new planning efforts in the
early 1970s in anticipation of slower growth in the 1980s (described in Chapter Four), a group of experienced administrative
staff in the systemwide office were assigned the task of determining how the new academic plan could be made operational
through resource management in other than a strict formula-
based mode. This effort introduced a series of concepts important to the management of the university's resources, including
modified program resource criteria, resource use assessment,
and decentralization of decisions within policy guidelines. It
also identified the need to elevate budgetary policy to a higher
administrative level, to refocus the budget and accounting operations, and to rethink the current management information systems. The Academic Planning and Program Review Board had
already begun to review campus budgets in the context of academic planning objectives. The board members hoped campuses
would set their own priorities for program development, since
as enrollment leveled off, resources would not likely be available to implement all their plans for development. They therefore sought to get the campuses to express their annual budget
requests in terms of resources needed to implement specific
planning goals. This attempt failed, partly because objectives
were still too broad to influence resource decisions, partly because the process was both static and mechanical, partly because
campus leaders feared prematurely exposing plans and options,
and partly because of disagreement over responsibility for the
design of the new resource management process.

These difficulties stemmed, in part, from several common
procedural flaws. For one, leaders at each campus sought to
guess what central university administrators would include as

priorities in the university's budget request to the state and to formulate campus priorities that would bring the most income to their campus, and they devoted much effort to "proving" that their campus was receiving the poorest allocations among the nine. For another, frank interchange was inadequate between campus and systemwide administrators about objectives, plans, programs, and resources, leaving too much authority in setting program priorities to staff at both the campus and systemwide levels. These staff members lacked the detailed understanding and experiences of academic operations needed to replace outmoded formulas with more sophisticated allocative standards for academic activities and with a more complex approach to other facets of resource management. Finally management information systems at the systemwide level were not designed to serve analytical needs, and the financial accounting system was of little help in financial analysis. As a result, the information base for developing new allocative standards was inadequate for setting program resource criteria and assessing progress toward objectives.

In the absence of both a shared sense of priorities and mechanisms to match these priorities to resource allocation decisions, frustration of faculty members and campus and systemwide administrators alike increased. Campuses preferred broader, less controlled allocations, while systemwide staff believed detailed program plans should be costed so that allocations would better match resource needs with program mix on each campus. Systemwide administrators agreed with the staff objective, but realistically could not and ideally should not allocate resources to individual operating units below the campus level. Yet to withdraw to a less controlled procedure required an audit capability that at the time did not exist and a management orientation far different from that in existence. The professional experience, creativity, and political sensitivity of staff were simply inadequate to the task of developing proposals for resource management approaches appropriate to a changing environment and decentralized decision making. Strongly influenced by existing state budgetary processes, budget staff in particular were largely control-oriented rather than policy-oriented.

Stage Two: Resource Management for Fiscal Stringency

In 1975, newly appointed President Saxon sought to strengthen the academic leadership of systemwide administration by appointing faculty members to several key administrative positions. Faculty members were appointed to direct development of university personnel policy and to represent the university to the state legislature and executive offices. A new academic vice-president was given broader planning responsibilities. The president also approved two studies of resource management and its relation to planning (1) how to improve, at reasonable cost, the quality and usefulness of information for campus and systemwide leaders and (2) how to clarify and update the roles and responsibilities of systemwide administrators in the university. The objective of these two studies was, in part, to improve total resource use in meeting the university's planning objectives.

These studies highlighted major improvements that university officials could make to improve the university's ability to deal with an uncertain and increasingly challenging future. They opened the way for significant changes in the process, organization, and staffing of resource management and, in particular, of supporting financial services. The changes made included:

- Development of information and analysis of planning assumptions, options, and risks to guide decision making.
- A new planning resource calendar (illustrated in Chapter Four) that established schedules for internal planning and resource management decisions rather than merely acquisition and allocation of new resources.
- A new mode of interaction between systemwide and campus administrators, away from a formal, written annual budget exchange and toward an ongoing informal discussion of planning and program issues, with most resource decisions following agreements on program changes.
- Systemwide administrative commitment of funds beyond the present budget year to add certainty to campus decision making and to reinforce the importance of program planning in the future.

- Refocusing current accounting and financial analysis activities in three ways: (1) estimating future resource levels to allow for forward commitments; (2) using funds from different sources as a total package to increase effectiveness of a given set of resources; and (3) allocating a majority of funds at one time in the planning cycle to further increase certainty.

These changes showed that academic programs—new or existing—could be developed and expanded without significant new money and that other programs could be reduced or eliminated by forward planning and managing resource transfers.

Stage Three: Resource Management for Uncertainty

To orchestrate the newly developed intermediate planning and resource management process, a "Resource Management Policy and Methodology" unit was created at the systemwide offices. This group consisted of six professional analysts, two administrative staff members, and three half-time graduate students. The unit worked with the three key vice-presidents responsible for planning, resources, and personnel. Its members guided and staffed the informal campus visits of systemwide officers recounted in Chapter Four; worked with the vice-presidents in identifying and analyzing issues and objectives, examining past patterns of resource use, projecting available funds and reserve levels to cover unexpected needs, and identifying long-term policy questions for appropriate bodies to study and resolve; and staffed discussions among the vice-presidents on implementing resource decisions.

As a "staff" rather than a "line" unit, the Resource Management Policy and Methodology unit provided the technical competence to gather information from disparate sources to help key administrators make necessary planning and resource decisions while ensuring that these managers retained control over these decisions. It could synthesize and integrate policy problems across functional boundaries. Because it was small it had to rely on faculty, staff, and administrative expertise throughout the university for information and assistance. It served as an educational tool for policy makers, but its small size reduced the possibility of developing into another centralized operating unit with excessive independence.

Estimating Future Income. To estimate future income, a task force of staff was drawn from all the systemwide offices managing funds. Because information on the status of funds had been dispersed, along with the responsibility for funds management, without adequate coordination throughout these offices, overall estimates of expected and current income flows were exceptionally conservative. As a result, each year actual income exceeded projections, and unexpected balances had invariably built up as the year progressed. This had resulted in less than optimum use of funds and in repeated questioning by campus leaders, external auditors, and legislative committees of the university's ability to manage its funds.

The task force, aided by a senior staff member from the resource management unit, (1) determined financial reserves, unexpended balances, and carry-forwards for all funds; (2) estimated actual income generated, including interest income for each fund source; (3) projected income at least five years into the future and explicitly specified all assumptions used in the projections; (4) matched currently planned expenditures against this expected income, differentiating between expenditures on the basis of (a) legal or contractual arrangements, (b) administrative or regental commitments, and (c) "traditional" or historical expenditure patterns where no formal commitment existed; (5) identified expected net balances available for use five years in the future; and (6) shared this information among central administrators.

Perhaps not surprisingly, enough uncommitted funds were discovered to develop reserves to meet unexpected resource stringencies and also allow some forward-year commitments. At the same time, serious potential declines in income from some sources were identified, which indicated the need to plan on less money from some sources in the future and the need for vigorous fund raising. For example, this analysis provided an early estimate of the potential impact on the university of the initia-

tive to limit property taxation in California, should it pass
(Proposition 13). With a sounder sense of what income was
available and likely to become available in the next several
years, multiyear resource plans to guide selective program
changes could be developed and resources committed in advance of the annual cycle. These multiyear allocations relieved
some campus uncertainties, tended to improve the efficiency
of resource use, diminished the impact of the annual budget
cycle, and let campus leaders focus additional attention on long-
term academic issues. In one case, simply informing two campuses that, following a small reduction in their base for reallocation to other campuses, no further reductions would be made
over the next two to three years resulted in their sharing more
information about their academic plans and strategies than had
been available in the previous eight.

Achieving Flexibility in Resource Use. To increase flexibility in the use of funds, the Resource Management Policy and
Methodology unit again adopted a task force approach to (1)
examine how individual funds had been managed historically,
(2) inventory current policies governing the use of available
funds, (3) outline the legal restrictions and policy constraints affecting fund uses and how these restrictions and constraints limited future management options, and (4) identify organizational
incentives and disincentives that affected fund management.
The unit recommended three criteria for fund use policies:

1. *Appropriateness of fund use to fund characteristics.* For
   example, unrestricted money should not be used on programs for which restricted money is available, and funds
   with widely fluctuating levels of income or an unstable future should not be committed for ongoing purposes, such
   as salaries. In many cases, funding sources were not well
   matched to program use.
2. *Flexibility in application.* For example, policies that do not
   allow for loans as well as appropriations from a given fund
   may result in suboptimal use of resources. Thus, a policy
   that provides money to students only for grants-in-aid is
   much less flexible and likely to meet the totality of student

needs than one that permits loans as well as grants. The same is true for capital expenditures.
3. *Legal and political defensibility.* Policies must not only meet the objectives of the university but also adhere to the purposes for which the funds were provided.

Using these criteria, the unit proposed new formal policies for major nonstate fund sources, including grant and contract overhead recovery. As an illustration, the "University Opportunity Fund," made up of the overhead recovered from federal grants and contracts, had originally been set up to stimulate creativity and scholarship in disciplines receiving little extramural support and to provide enrichment beyond state funding. But through years of incremental decisions devoted to meeting "current needs," the income from the Opportunity Fund had been diverted to fund high-priority current operations for which state funding had not been made available, such as increased police protection, correcting previously deferred plant maintenance, retaining the level of library acquisitions, and providing student financial aid. University officials believed that it was time to articulate carefully the responsibilities of the state for such activities as these and that the original purpose of the Opportunity Fund should be reinstated by using it to stimulate creativity and thus help the university remain at the cutting edge in teaching and learning.

The unit developed a policy that set two specific goals for the Opportunity Fund: (1) to stimulate extramural funding and (2) to provide for faculty development, including affirmative action and opportunities for research. This policy accomplished three purposes: First, it assured that some funds were earmarked to help meet the university's major academic objectives of vitality and quality. Second, it provided a rationale against which programs presently supported by the Opportunity Fund could be reviewed and judged on their merit in fulfilling these objectives and its goals. Third, it provided a basis against which state funding responsibilities could be more effectively presented and defended.

Decentralizing Resource Management. To institute what

amounted to the most radical of the changes in resource management practices—the shift from precontrols to a decentralized decision mode with a postaudit capability—several experimental policies were introduced to learn about how such policies could guide decisions. One of these experiments was called the "Ten Percent Policy." Rather than controlling campus decisions over faculty appointments in advance by requiring, for instance, that they hire new faculty only on a "temporary" basis in order to retain flexibility, the Ten Percent Policy required that each campus establish the capability to relinquish 10 percent of its regular ladder-rank faculty positions on one year's notice. The campuses could meet this policy in any manner they chose. They could earmark positions as temporary if they wanted; they could use deaths, retirements, and resignations; they could offer two-year contracts to junior faculty members—so long as 10 percent of their faculty positions could be freed with a year's notice. This policy met the goal of achieving flexibility in faculty members to meet unexpected fluctuations in funding; at the same time it avoided the disincentives inherent in precontrol of specific positions.

A second experiment in moving from a precontrolling line-item budget to more flexible objective-oriented resource management was initiated in conjunction with the University Opportunity Fund. First, current line-item expenditures from this fund were aggregated under the two broad objectives specified in the new policy, and campuses were given the choice of using these resources in continuing to fund activities they deemed presently committed or reallocating the money to activities they felt were of higher priority as long as these activities fell within the policy objectives. This provided them the opportunity to terminate low-priority, line-item expenditures and to shift resources to achieve desired program changes. Second, the campuses were given three years to develop a plan for how these funds were to be used to meet the objectives stated for the fund and to specify the criteria and means for assessing whether these objectives were being realized. Upon completion of the plans the systemwide office proposed allocating a "lump sum" to each campus from this fund. The campuses would have flexibility in using Opportunity Fund income as long as they accomplished agreed-on objectives.

A third new practice designed to encourage movement toward objective-policy-oriented resource decisions was a revised form for conveying agreements between systemwide and campus administrators on policy and program goals, resources allocated to help achieve those goals, the length of time for which resources would be made available, and the degree of certainty attached to future allocations. The following letter signed by the president to a campus chancellor, regarding final resource decisions, illustrates one way in which university officers used resource decisions to relate performance more closely to planning goals and to move away from precontrol toward increased campus flexibility in using money to further policy.

Dear Colleagues:

I am transmitting to you under separate cover a summary of resource decisions and planning parameters covering the current planning and resource management cycle. These include the commitments for this period transmitted to you by the vice-president in his recent letter, tentative allocations for 1977-78 for all programs from all funds, and planning targets for 1978-79 which will serve as the basis for development of the regents' budget.

This year, I believe we have made significant progress in developing new resource management processes to meet our academic objectives. First, through the series of discussions with you, understanding of campus academic plans and resource needs is improved. A multiyear approach in resource planning to provide greater certainty to the planning environment is nearing the implementation phase. All funds are being used, in an integrated manner, to provide some additional resources for highest-priority needs such as libraries and academic support and to take advantage of special opportunities to improve quality when they present themselves. In addition, some policy changes have been effected to provide greater flexibility to the campuses in the management of their resources and changes made in budget processes to reduce unnecessary workload for both the campus and systemwide staff.

In providing commitments to you, we are guaranteeing those minimum levels of support independent of acquisition of additional state resources. Some of these commitments are only for one year, some are continuing. The target allocations for 1977-78 for those areas of the budget not covered by previous commitments (mostly supporting programs for this year) will be made firm after the final budget act is signed July 1.

Within the next couple of years, the intent is that allocations will be made only once each year and those funding levels will be guaranteed as was done with the commitments made this year. Understanding of campus resource needs in all programs must be improved and better procedures for estimating income must be developed before this step can be taken.

The 1978-79 planning targets which were included in the attached allocation document were developed by estimates of probable levels of new resources, from analysis of past campus budget statements, and by use of existing criteria and formulas where appropriate. 1978-79 planning targets are not complete because many decisions, for example, libraries, are still open. Some of these decisions, for example, organized research, await campus response; others await further systemwide action. Work will continue with the campuses to resolve these over the next six weeks.

For the future, an objective is to provide planning targets for a three-year period in even broader categories (for example, instruction, research, and supporting programs) to allow adjustment across functional categories before budgets are finalized. This will provide increased planning certainty and greater campus flexibility in the assignment of resources to areas of greatest need, both to bring about over the next several years a budget which is a better reflection of how funds are to be spent and to examine the appropriateness of current budget control points and categories. This greater flexibility will only be possible when clear resource policy and a process for agreeing on our specific objectives ahead of time and following progress toward them are in place.

A major change in management of university funds is the allocation of all of these funds as is being done now in the budget allocation cycle rather than after the final budget decisions have been made. This is to let you know as soon as possible what your total resources are likely to be. These allocations from university funds must remain tentative for 1977-78 until we obtain regental approval in July 1977. In the future, allocations from these funds can be considered firm once allocated, for action on university fund expenditures will be taken earlier in the year.

Also this year, a new set of objectives for the use of university funds is being developed. University funds have always been earmarked to provide resources needed to attain the margin of quality in our teaching and research programs which make this university a truly distinguished one. Because of the stringency of state general funds in recent years, university funds have gone increasingly to meet core needs of campus operations. This has removed to a large extent one of the few flexible sources of funds available, a flexibility which is going to become increasingly important as growth slows and marginal resources associated with that growth decline. Much thought has been given not only to how to continue to provide these needed resources to preserve and enhance campus flexibility in resource use but also to how university funds can be channeled to meet today's needs for quality assurance and to take advantage of a few real targets of opportunity.

While a new funding policy is not fully implemented, our objective is that at the end of two years the major university fund should support these following important academic objectives: (1) to provide adequate support for contract and grant administration and to move over time to return more of these funds to the campuses which have generated them; (2) to attract additional extramural funding, particularly on campuses that are not currently receiving adequate extramural research funding; and (3) to assure more nearly adequate professional opportunities in both teaching and research for faculty and students.

Additional work must be done at the systemwide level before this funding policy can be fully implemented. For 1977-78, however, some important steps have been taken to enhance your ability to use university funds to meet these needs on your campus. University funds have been identified in two categories. The first category is those programs for which funding is earmarked to assure implementation of policies and programs. These programs are affirmative action, instructional improvement, financial aid administration, parts of the intercampus exchange program, deferred maintenance, interim funding for the health sciences tuition offset, and the Data System of Instructional Resources and provision accounts. In the second category, the remainder of funds provided to your campus from university funds is available for allocation to you to enable the campus to go as far as possible in meeting the academic objectives for which the funds are being provided.

The difficulty in moving many of these resources, particularly in the short period of time, is recognized. However, adjustments that you care to make this year toward the above objectives are encouraged. You are being asked to provide a description of how these broad objectives will be made operational including allocation of funds to specific programs. Details are given on the attached schedule of university funds, and procedures for allocation are outlined in the forthcoming budget instructions. Let me again remind you, however, that in the absence of adequate means of assessing progress toward objectives, I must ask that you adhere very tightly to the intent for which these funds are provided. After the means of assessing progress are established, a greater degree of campus flexibility will be possible.

There are many important academic policy and resource issues which have been left unresolved in 1977-78 that will become high priorities for 1978-79. These include new programs to enhance instruction, implementation of the library plan, and development of a sound policy for campus research programs. State support for additional acquisitions has not been forthcoming for the past several years. This year, in recognition of library needs, university funds have been provided for book acquisitions. Full state acceptance and funding of the library plan is a top priority for 1978-79. The careful attention which has been given in the case of libraries to articulating a systemwide funding policy consistent with our academic objectives is an example of the way other major areas will be approached as resource management is more clearly related to academic planning.

Serious thought is being given to how we can better support instructional improvement. A proposed policy for a teaching sabbatical leave to focus on improving the instructional process is one such means of assuring continued quality instruction. This remains a high priority. We should be ready with policy and funding proposals no later than 1979-80.

Development of a systemwide funding policy for research is another major priority for 1978-79. We have several important objectives for our research program which need to be supported by resource management policies. The most important is to enhance and maintain our research capability. Funding programs responsive to the needs of individual campuses need to be developed in order to accomplish this. For some campuses, returning a greater percentage of funds recovered for indirect costs will be most important. For other campuses, providing resources to develop greater capability to attract extramural funds will be essential. Finally, for all campuses, we will need to improve support for research in those areas where extramural funding may not be as easily available: the arts and humanities, for junior faculty, and for graduate students. Maintenance of a dynamic and well-integrated research program is always a high priority for a quality university. The next few months will be used to prepare a strong request for increases in state funding for research for 1978-79.

I hope you are as enthusiastic about our progress and future objectives as I am. The instructions for budget preparation are being sent directly to your budget officer under separate cover, along with more detailed schedules.

Sincerely,

President

Reducing Staff Workload. These new mechanisms for transmitting resource decisions helped relate policy decisions to actual dollar allocations, but the Resource Management Policy and Methodology unit soon discovered that new mechanisms were also needed to track income estimates, resource commitments, planning targets, and timing of allocations. As these data needs emerged, several new management information systems were proposed—among them a computer-based financial projection model, a computer-based financial recordkeeping system, and a new accounting system. Once these systems were in place, it was expected that staff workload could be reduced in the traditional budget and finance areas. The major reasons were two: First, staff work in preparing and analyzing resource needs was reduced as these needs were identified during planning discussions. Thus, staff work focused on specific issues and problems identified in these discussions rather than being dissipated on what in the past had often turned out to be peripheral issues. Second, allocating all funds at one time each year also reduced workloads because campus demands for additional resources to meet "new" or unanticipated needs over the year diminished— resource distribution was no longer a year-round task.

Ensuring Faculty Participation in Resource Management. With tighter resources and accompanying skepticism among the faculty about the wisdom of many budget decisions, more formal means for broadening the base of faculty advice on resource management were desirable.

Each of the campuses was left largely on its own to develop means of responding to changing resource management processes. But systemwide officials sought to make sure that on each campus faculty members were consulted and involved in campus planning and encouraged their participation in resource decision processes.

The pattern on the Davis campus illustrates this overall policy. Davis had instituted an Academic Planning Council chaired by the chancellor and consisting of members of his staff, faculty, and students. One of its responsibilities was to help guide the chancellor's planning decisions. For greater faculty involvement in the planning and resource management process, however, the campus Academic Senate in 1977 formed a six-member faculty committee on Academic Planning and Budget Review. Among its other duties, the committee was charged by the senate (1) to confer with and (2) to advise the chancellor and divisional administrators regarding policy on academic planning and budget and faculty allocations and to initiate studies of existing and proposed academic programs as they related to campus planning, budget, and resource allocations. The committee recommended to the chancellor early on that academic quality should be the first consideration in suggesting program and resource changes—with resource use effectiveness an important consideration as well.

Some deans expressed substantial skepticism about a faculty committee engaging in such studies and offering advice to them, viewing the faculty activities as encroaching on the deans' own management responsibilities. Some faculty members were uneasy also, particularly in departments where workloads had declined or previous program reviews had pointed out weaknesses. But senior administrators withheld public judgment, pending sufficient evidence that the committee could contribute consistently and responsibly to the decision process.

During its first three years, the committee, with the help of discipline-oriented subcommittees, collected and examined selected information on each academic department and program to determine current staffing levels and projected turnover, instructional workloads, graduate and undergraduate student enrollment trends, support funds, teaching assistants and other instructional personnel other than those with professorial titles. Program quality evaluations, where available, contributed to summary statements about quality of departmental programs. The committee then drafted a report pointing out academic strengths and weaknesses and reviewing resource use in all academic programs, noting where additional academic positions were needed as well as where some might be found on campus for transfer to other uses.

The committee sent the draft to the chancellor, who had it reviewed for accuracy by deans and other administrators. Portions were also reviewed by the appropriate departments or programs to ensure correct information about them. The draft brought forth a broad array of responses, but most important, the chancellor and senior administrators found that faculty involvement could point the way to improved resource use; that objective expertise of faculty members could be brought to bear on major questions of reallocation, program quality, and faculty workload; and that a faculty committee could make recommendations of a kind many administrative officers might find politically difficult.

Qualitative judgments about programs were not universally well received, and when the committee suggested that resources were not as fully employed as they could be, the use of traditional workload measures was not accepted. Yet the overall reaction to the committee's work was positive. It was clearly established that faculty could contribute most effectively to planning and resource allocation decisions by combining quality assessment with a sophisticated perspective on resource use.

The draft report accomplished enough that the committee then undertook three more tasks: (1) improving the accuracy and timeliness of information about all campus operating units, (2) developing an ongoing review process to advise the chancellor on the allocation and reallocation of faculty positions, and (3) providing ongoing advice to the chancellor on resource planning and allocation. Figure 4 illustrates the second of these three efforts. It reproduces part of the committee's report on recommended procedures for allocating and reallocating faculty positions—an approach that was tested and, with modifications, adopted. To accomplish the third task, the committee established six guiding premises on its proper contributions to resource decisions:

1. The Committee on Academic Planning and Budget Review (CAPBR) can influence campus resource allocations over time most effectively by involving itself in budgetary planning issues and critiquing the budgetary process on the campus.
2. Immediate allocation decisions must be made by administrative officers who have the authority and responsibility for such actions.
3. The immediate decisions can be best influenced by careful longer-term analysis and budgetary planning decisions.
4. For CAPBR to be effective in budget activity, it must build a reputation for providing resource-planning guidance to the campus administration.
5. Second-guessing administrative decisions will destroy the necessary interaction between the faculty and administration, without which CAPBR will be incapable of serving the campus effectively.
6. CAPBR should select two or three initial resource planning issues for intensive study, work closely with the administration to clarify the information base, and provide as objective and penetrating analysis as it can develop.

The initial study area proposed by the committee and agreed to by the administration was the use and distribution of teaching assistants and other auxiliary teaching personnel. The need for this study emerged during the committee's review with members of the administration of the campus's annual "target budget." The study objective was to develop a set of targets for possible reallocation of these positions among departments over a three- to four-year period. Other studies now under consideration are (1) relative levels of academic support by discipline, (2) funding levels for specific aspects of institutional support, and (3) the adequacy of the budgetary planning process in guiding short-term allocation decisions, assessing the results achieved, and adjusting budgetary targets. Additional objectives of the committee are to assist other faculty groups in review of both undergraduate and graduate programs.

Originally questioned as unnecessary or inappropriate, the committee has become an accepted and important element in the planning, resource management, and assessment cycle at Davis. Continuing acceptance will depend on the committee's ability to attract interested, dedicated, and experienced faculty. Continuing effectiveness, in turn, will depend on committee members investing a substantial amount of time. Although members are understandably tempted to obtain staff assistance to help cope with the workload, the committee as a whole has strongly resisted this procedure. The argument is that support from institution staff may result in the committee losing control over its activities—and that it might be perceived as an extension of the administration, rather than as an autonomous group with the perspective and credibility necessary to do its job well.

Conclusion

Implementing decentralized multiyear resource management such as that illustrated in this chapter by the experience of the University of California requires sufficient time to educate everyone concerned. Its concepts depart so significantly from conventional wisdom in the administration of public colleges and universities that it elicits extensive questioning, if not

Figure 4. Review Process for Position Allocation.

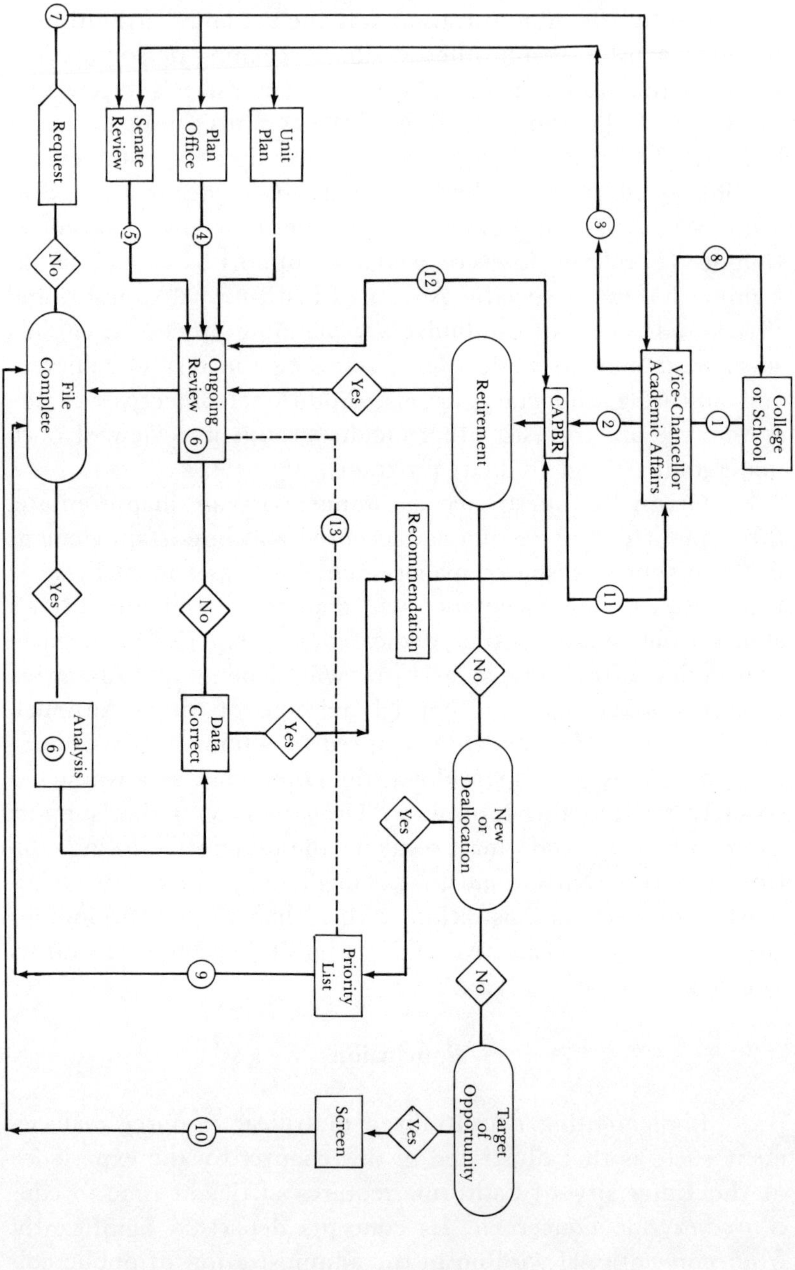

Committee on Academic Planning and Budget Review (CAPBR) Recommendations on Review Process for Position Allocations

The attached chart has been prepared to assist CAPBR and the administration in providing pertinent, timely, and useful advice on planning questions related to faculty FTE and to specific allocation proposals. The process can be used for planning exercises as well as actual allocations.

The chart is not an organizational chart in which the boxes represent specific groups. It is intended to illustrate a process for dealing with questions, and as a result the lines generally represent information paths and the figures represent questions, functions, actions, or groups.

The numbered circles are keys to the explanations for the specific pathways, which are given in the following paragraphs.

1. Requests for FTE allocation and justification forwarded to chancellor. In addition, notification of deaths, resignations, retirements, and targets of opportunity are forwarded to the chancellor's office. CAPBR will not be involved in this step.

2. The chancellor's office provides CAPBR as early in the fall as possible or as the information becomes available:

   a. Retirements—those anticipated and the departments in which they occur. (Notification as they occur and annually.)

   b. Resignations—departments in which they occur and whether the position has reverted to the department or has been retained by the dean. (Notification as they occur and annually.)

   c. New positions or deallocations—(Notification of the number as soon as they are known.)

   d. Targets of opportunity—Notification of requesting department, area to be covered, CV of the candidate, and where FTE will come from. (Notification as soon as request is received.)

   e. Conversions—Notification of positions converted from temporary to permanent positions and where position is to be located. (Notification at the time the conversion takes place.)

   f. Failure to make tenure—These positions always revert to the department; hence CAPBR does not consider these positions as candidates for alternative recommendation. However, for informational purposes CAPBR wishes to be informed when and where such positions occur.

3. Unit plan and reviews—CAPBR requests up-to-date unit plans and new plans as they are submitted. In addition, we request all reviews conducted by the colleges or done by outside agencies. This pathway will also carry responses to requests for additional information.

4. Planning Office input—CAPBR will work with the Planning Office to obtain data from the existing computer files, including enrollments, FTE load, teaching load, and so forth.

5. Senate review—All unit reviews, both graduate and undergraduate, will become part of the file.

6. The ongoing review and analysis steps will be done by persons or groups designated by CAPBR. This could be, for example, CAPBR as a whole, a single designated person, or an ad hoc committee or other mechanisms as appropriate.

7. Request—The request is for additional information. CAPBR will interact directly with the Planning Office and Academic Senate. Requests for additional information which must come from the units will be forwarded through the chancellor's office.

8. Request—The chancellor's office will forward requests for new information to the dean or unit involved.

9. New positions or deallocations—The ongoing review process must include continuing awareness of areas on campus which should receive priority in allocation or deallocation. The recommendation from here may simply identify a slate of departments as candidates. The priority list narrows the number of files which must be examined. If the files seem complete, the subsequent process follows the route for retirements.

10. Target of opportunity—They will have to be handled on a case-by-case basis but will involve an initial screening based on the candidate, area, and department plan.

11. Recommendations to chancellor's office.

12. This pathway designates the fact that the CAPBR and the ongoing review process are in close communication and, in fact, the ongoing review is one of the functions of CAPBR.

13. The priority list is a product of the ongoing review process. It is expected that, as a result of review, priority and problem areas will be identified. This list will tend to focus allocation/deallocation questions into those areas which are most appropriate.

suspicion. Complete implementation of the resource management approach presented requires overcoming some administrative fears that more open and rational internal management of all resources than is usually practiced would result in reduced state appropriations and further attempts by the state to control nonstate funds held by the university. These fears had led some administrators to safeguard information excessively.

Educating all concerned means convincing department chairs and faculty that uncertainty about the future and about available resources can be reduced to a point at which forward-year commitments can be relied upon and these personnel can make decisions on them. Because the new approach to resource management requires fewer people but different skills in budget and financial management, it usually means retraining the existing staff, whose traditional activities are changed and who are sometimes less than eager to accept a new role. Administrative staff who generally think in programmatic terms quickly see the merits of the change, but those who are primarily process- and control-oriented are anxious about moving away from the old procedures, particularly because reduction in routine workload, demands for new analytical skills, and a more academic orientation threaten many of them.

The new approach means educating and involving faculty in the resource management process while avoiding bureaucratizing the process by overparticipation. It means educating the governing board, for their approval will probably be required for several major policy changes, particularly the use of various nonstate funds. Finally, it involves educating the state bureaucracy. Many senior state officials understand the need for a new resource management approach and generally favor its adoption, but state agency staff members tend to see a loss of longstanding interaction with university staff as a loss of influence and, for many, as a challenge to their jobs.

Beyond these tasks, and beyond the introduction of new practices described thus far in this book, further implementation of multiyear resource management concepts requires changes in institutional assessment and evaluation. Allowing departments and other units greater latitude in using the resources they are allocated to meet agreed-on goals means instituting postexpenditure assessment of their progress toward these goals. This third major element in the management cycle rounds out the planning-resource management-assessment process and is the topic of the next two chapters.

8

Assessing
Performance
for Successful
Management

Planning and resource management without expanded assessment of performance and results can improve college and university administration only marginally. To round out the management cycle requires at least a five-part assessment process, involving the review of (1) academic programs, (2) administrative and academic support services, (3) personnel performance, (4) resource use, and (5) policy. All five facets of assessment must be carried on routinely; assessment results must then be used for the reconsideration of plans and possible redirection of resources as illustrated in Figure 5.

The review of an academic program, for example, may indicate that it can be raised to true distinction with a key faculty appointment. The review of an administrative service such as campus planning may reveal that, although adequate for the

Figure 5. Evaluation.

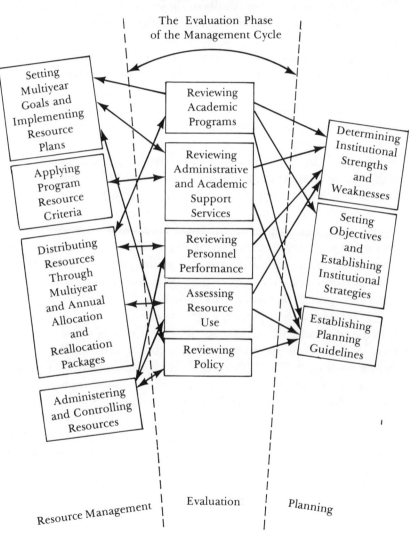

The Evaluation Phase
of the Management Cycle

Setting Multiyear Goals and Implementing Resource Plans

Reviewing Academic Programs

Determining Institutional Strengths and Weaknesses

Applying Program Resource Criteria

Reviewing Administrative and Academic Support Services

Setting Objectives and Establishing Institutional Strategies

Distributing Resources Through Multiyear and Annual Allocation and Reallocation Packages

Reviewing Personnel Performance

Assessing Resource Use

Reviewing Policy

Establishing Planning Guidelines

Administering and Controlling Resources

Resource Management

Evaluation

Planning

past, it is poorly oriented for meeting current problems. Such information is important in determining institutional strengths and weaknesses, informing planning, and setting priorities. Unfortunately, however, the results of these reviews are rarely linked in this manner to subsequent decisions. Frequently, information stops with the department involved or a dean or director, if not with those conducting the reviews. Personnel reviews other than of academics usually meet a similar fate. Information on the productivity and competence of personnel must be generated and fed into the planning and resource management system to induce desired changes. Similarly, data on current resource use must be available to induce midcourse corrections in resource use during a budget period. In a decentralized management system, where departments and other operating units have extensive flexibility in budgeting and spending resources as a means of improving efficiency in obtaining objectives, they require timely information on current fiscal balances for all sources of income. Quarterly or semiannual after-the-fact reports from the accounting office are inadequate. Finally, institutional policies need periodic review to assure that they implement institutional objectives and goals rather than impeding their attainment.

Most academic leaders are experienced in assessing the quality of academic programs, the effectiveness of administrative and academic support services, and the performance of academic personnel. These three aspects of the assessment process are well-established management activities, and this chapter begins by discussing these familiar assessment practices in the context of planning and resource management. But academic administrators are far less familiar with techniques of the other two areas of assessment—resource use and policy—needed to support the management cycle. Later sections of the chapter therefore suggest what form these new assessment activities might take and how they might be developed.

Broadening the Scope of Academic Program Review

Until the middle 1970s, academic program review was concerned predominantly with quality control (Lee and Bowen, 1975). Both existing and new program proposals were evaluated.

Review of existing programs was ad hoc, concentrating on those programs known to be deficient academically. On the basis of the plans for proposed curricula, degrees, or departments, additions were either approved, deferred until revised, or denied. Since the middle 1970s, however, program review activities have expanded in at least four ways: (1) to determine the resources needed for new programs—for example, what particular faculty expertise and support services will be required in order for a program to develop and contribute to institutional vitality; (2) to examine how efficiently and effectively resources are being used in existing programs, including whether excessive "duplication" or "redundancy" exists; (3) to correct specific weaknesses, identify areas of overexpansion, and highlight resource deficiencies; and (4) to guide program retrenchment by providing a basis for determining which programs should be reduced in scope or phased out if resource stringencies become severe or campus priorities dictate reallocation. The implications of these expansions in the purposes and uses of program review are far-reaching. Program review is now more formal, more frequent, and more comprehensive in scope and depth than in the past. Program review has expanded to periodic formal reevaluation of all programs. The criteria used to judge the operation of existing programs have changed substantially from those used in the past to judge only program quality. And the procedures and personnel involved have grown in number and complexity.

As an example, review criteria for approving undergraduate instructional programs during the growth period focused primarily on the appropriateness of the educational objectives of the program, scope of the curriculum and instruction, competence of the teaching staff, and adequacy of procedures used in evaluating teaching. In contrast, criteria for reviewing an existing program include its contribution to institutional mission, its relation to the academic program core of the campus, the need for the program in light of sustained student interest, its potential sources and levels of support, its efficiency in the use of assigned resources, including current and projected faculty workload, and its distribution of faculty by age and rank to determine future turnover. Today, program review may judge not merely quality or the program's contribution to institutional objectives but also cost—not only in terms of effectiveness but also of efficiency.

Inadequacy of Past Review Practices. Since the process of reviewing programs for quality has been widely understood and well accepted, administrators have tended to continue existing review procedures despite these broader focuses. Adding efficiency criteria to existing review processes—which were designed to assess only program quality—has meant more work for faculty and staff. It has also introduced an additional array of complex interpersonal dynamics among faculty who serve on review committees. During growth, reviews of existing programs were traditionally self-studies, initiated at the department, division, or faculty senate level. As growth slowed or stopped some faculty members have been reluctant to encourage or engage in reviews of ongoing programs that may lead to adverse decisions on program scope or funding. Faculty reluctance has shifted some of the burden for these reviews to administrative offices and has led to centralizing and standardizing of review procedures and decisions.

Combining the objectives of judging both quality and efficiency in the same process is not optimal. To do so may compromise the integrity of existing review processes designed to judge program quality, reduce chances of obtaining objective evaluations of resource use, and limit the acceptability of findings of review for both purposes. A broader array of evaluative processes, as well as new criteria, is required for the assessment of program performance. Developing resource use assessments and policy reviews as evaluative processes separate but parallel to program review, as described later in this chapter, can help avoid some of the pitfalls of combining multiple-objective reviews in a single action. Program reviews for quality must be conducted by faculty members knowledgeable about the relevant discipline(s) of the program. When reviewing programs for efficiency, faculty members must be included not only for their disciplinary knowledge but to avoid the appearance that resource reviews are the sole responsibility of the administration.

Establishing systematic procedures and criteria to guide program reviews that may lead to program discontinuance should be developed before such action is required, to avoid the danger of ad hoc processes and crisis decisions. The procedures should be integrated into ongoing review activities. When a program must be reduced or eliminated, the criteria on which the decision is made must be sufficiently explicit and the evaluative procedures sufficiently detailed that the action can be justified to any reasonable observer. Without such criteria and guidelines, necessary action can be seriously delayed or thwarted by partisan opposition. With them, conflict cannot be eliminated, but the debate can be contained and focused on substantive issues.

The best program review efforts exist in those institutions where faculty and administrators have clarified responsibility for both the reviews and the decisions resulting from review, where the faculty's critical role in program review is recognized by administrators even if they retain some concern over the role of faculty in advising on specific resource allocation decisions, and where both faculty and administrators have begun to grapple with the difficult issue of how to balance qualitative judgments with quantitative information in reaching these decisions. Many of the best efforts have occurred at the graduate school level, spurred primarily by graduate deans as they have become concerned over the vitality and breadth of particular programs, the quality of admittees, the time involved to earn a degree, and the placement of graduates.

Needed Improvements. Program reviews need to be designed to encourage rather than discourage change. Thus, existing programs should be evaluated regularly, since the resulting changes are more likely to be gradual than shattering and will ensure performance that meets current needs efficiently and effectively. Routine review will also minimize external influences on the choice of programs or the criteria to be used for review.

Second, since "quality" and "excellence" are such key criteria in program review, greater specificity of these criteria regarding academic vigor and rigor are essential, recognizing, of course, that absolute standards are suspect and any standard

must be defined and interpreted in the context of specific reviews. At the time reviews are initiated, those responsible must
explicitly define (1) the criteria they expect to be used, (2) the
scope of judgments and recommendations they need, (3) the
sources of information to be employed and how they can be
introduced into the review process, and (4) the likely uses of
the results. Quality of both the reviews and their recommendations will improve, since reviewers will be more realistic, specific, and politically sensitive in the advice they provide because
they will understand the broader dimensions of assessment of
which their review activities are a part.

   Third, administrators and faculty leaders must eliminate
all duplicative review efforts and must protect faculty and staff
time to the fullest extent possible within the constraint of conducting adequate reviews. Deciding how responsibility for reviews is to be shared between faculty and administration not
only avoids wasted effort of separate faculty senate and admin-
istrator-initiated reviews but focuses attention on the interrelationship of quality and cost. Shared responsibility also avoids
the danger of implying that administrators are interested only in
resource-use assessments that concern efficiency, while faculty
should deal only with quality assessments of program effectiveness.

   Through such improvements, program reviews can become more specific, less time-consuming, better documented,
and more directed to needed action than in the past. Reports
from such reviews will increasingly contain information on such
issues as trends in the quality of students being admitted, characteristics and attributes of the faculty, and scope and quality
of course offerings, as well as recommendations on specific marginal resource changes that can make substantial qualitative differences in the programs.

   The impact of such reviews can be illustrated by the experience of a large Midwestern public university system. During
only one year in the latter half of the 1970s, program reviews
resulted in the following actions:

• Nine programs received recommendations calling for additional faculty to meet increasing workloads attributable to

growing enrollments, while three others received recommendations that faculty resources be reduced.

- Twenty received recommendations for curricular modification, consideration of program restructuring, or merger or redirection of new program thrusts.
- Seven were directed to improve the balance among their course offerings and to improve course scheduling.
- Five received recommendations that they make efforts to increase enrollments.
- Six received recommendations to change admission or evaluation standards.
- Five received recommendations calling for improved facilities or equipment.
- Thirty-one were made subject to continuing review.
- Twenty-one were recommended for phaseout; one was merged with another; and one was placed on inactive status pending further study.

The realization that self-evaluation and peer assessments can assist with these difficult decisions has generated enthusiasm for program review among both faculty and administrators. The latter also see the advantages of reviews to inform decisions. They also see the educational benefit to faculty from participating in the process. Reviews help ensure that difficult program choices are carefully weighed before action is taken, thus assuring faculty that decisions to cut or terminate programs are based on thorough information. Sharing the findings and recommendations appropriately makes the results available for review both by the affected units and by administrators and faculty leaders in campuswide planning and resource management discussions and decisions. In the campuswide context, program review recommendations are crucial to the total management process.

Expanding the Review of Administrative and Academic Supporting Services

Colleges and universities tend to be less rigorous in their management of administrative units, compared with other organizations. The reason seems to be that the arguments for "complexity of intellectual endeavors" and "creative freedom" advanced for academic departments are allowed to apply to administrative activities as well. These attitudes obstruct the sound management of administrative and academic support units. Neither complex intellectual endeavor nor creative freedom is essential to effective routine administrative operations. Specific standards for workload, job performance, and unit costs can improve effectiveness of administrative and academic support services, and they are fully appropriate for these units.

Increasingly, central administrative offices, student service units, libraries, computer services, plant maintenance and operation, budget offices, accounting systems, and other administrative and support services are becoming the subject of evaluation. Craven (1980) believes evaluation of these activities will soon become as common as review of academic programs. So many resources of colleges and universities are committed to administrative services that confining assessment to teaching and research programs alone restricts substantial opportunities for improved overall resource management. Equally important, in the absence of standards and information about the performance of administrative and support units, some institutions have cut these activities too deeply; these deep cuts have seriously compromised both the quality and level of services and have reduced the productivity of faculty and administrators as well. It is not a good use of resources for faculty members to type their own correspondence, for administrators to do their own filing, or for either to spend time cleaning offices. Careful evaluation of services is needed to determine where real efficiencies could occur.

Because time continually widens the gap between what is and what should be adequate service, the lack of routine administrative review makes occasional ad hoc review more threatening when it does take place and intensifies the stress associated with the resulting necessary changes. Therefore, continued self-study, encouraged by senior administrators as a regular part of the management process, can uncover opportunities for improved service in a positive context. Those involved become more active contributors to planned improvements, and anxiety about resulting expansions and contractions of administrative units is reduced.

In addition, efficiencies in administrative and academic support services not only free resources for high-priority academic goals and objectives but can encourage faculty efficiency as well. Many faculty members are inherently suspicious about expenditures for administrative purposes. As a result, prudent administrators do not recommend reductions in academic programs or increases in faculty effort without being able to show that administrative and support activities have been exhaustively scrutinized, prudently trimmed, and efficiently streamlined. Tough evaluation of all institutional activities and demonstrated cost savings are always of benefit to institutions in making the argument for resources from funding agencies and potential donors. In some cases, public universities have been able to retain savings and use them for new purposes when administrators have convinced state officials that the savings were generated by greater efficiency as a result of self-study.

The evaluation of library operations illustrates changes that can reduce costs and increase effectiveness. One such study resulted in the development of new computerized cataloguing and automated acquisition processes. A substantial capital investment was required but, in the long run, the investment achieved enough savings to enable current acquisition and circulation staff levels to handle an increasing volume. Construction and acquisition of low-cost storage facilities for little-used material avoided costs of continued additions of expensive library space. Quality was enhanced because more resources could be used for purchasing new library materials rather than for servicing little-used material. By taking long-term costs into account, the study recommended against cutting the hours the library was open, eliminating retrospective purchases of journals and out-of-print books, or cutting down on reference staff—all of which would have provided short-term savings but resulted in long-term loss of service.

Other colleges and universities are finding alternative cost-effective methods of obtaining administrative and academic support services, such as using self-insurance for selected activities, contracting with outside vendors for needed services, and purchasing supplies cooperatively through consortia. Cost-benefit analysis can avoid mistaken efforts at cost saving, such as using inexpensive paint if buildings have to be repainted twice as frequently or buying inexpensive duplicating paper if it clogs machines and results in wasted paper and staff time.

Administrative units should be evaluated to see whether they are meeting changing needs, goals, and objectives. In one case, the assessment of business operations found that the basic functions of the business office were necessary but its effort to check transactions initiated by departments and other units to assure correctness was outmoded. Such checking had been necessary when department heads had not yet developed the capability for independent budget work, but times had changed although the operations had not. As a result of the review, the business office shifted its attention to developing cost-savings techniques or finding less expensive contractors for services.

In addition, some administrators are using evaluation to determine how productivity can be enhanced even with a reduced work force. After one university, which had cut its maintenance and janitorial staff severely, evaluated the subsequent productivity of remaining personnel, it hired a small number of new supervisors. Staff productivity increased and the quality of work improved dramatically.

Five major mechanisms can trigger evaluations of administrative and support units: (1) initiating cost studies of each unit; (2) calling for an update of unit plans and objectives; (3) undertaking financial or management audits; (4) reviewing current standards of work performance or asking for new ones to be developed; and (5) reviewing current administrative policy.

Outside assessments seem to be most helpful in the face of strong internal disagreements among staff over workload and staffing issues or when managers are contemplating a substantial and potentially controversial reorganization of a unit. Outside reviews may be essential to gain a needed degree of objectivity and to overcome some of the otherwise personal connotations that extensive change may hold.

Administrators are increasingly conscious of the need to separate review of units from review of individuals. Ongoing self-study facilitates this separation and reduces the tendency for staff to become so identified with a given activity that their performance cannot be separated from that of the unit. Effective staff should not be judged harshly and unfairly because of organizational weakness.

Assessing Personnel Performance

Both internal and external forces have influenced the scope and character of personnel performance review in recent years. Internal influences have included student interest in faculty evaluation, slowed growth and tighter resources, and the possibility of layoff. Among outside pressures, federal affirmative action regulations, laws to protect and enhance employee rights, court decisions regarding due process, and the possibility or presence of collective bargaining have resulted in more systematic and formal procedures.

Faculty Evaluation. Colleges and universities are now keeping detailed and formal records of faculty evaluation. These procedures require greater staff support than in the past, and faculty members must spend additional time keeping their own performance records and reviewing their colleagues' achievements. Also, administrative time is required to record the outcome of reviews at all administrative levels and for all job applicants, and some institutions require written justification for any negative personnel decision. Little debate arises over the goal of careful and equitable decisions or even the commitment of time and supporting resources. More hotly debated than the goal is the question whether candor in appraisal has been partly sacrificed in the process. Greater formality puts internal peer review to the test and sometimes results in difficult cases being passed upward for administrative decision without the benefit of candid peer review. In contrast, nearly everyone agrees that involving all ranks of faculty in departmental evaluations is improving peer review. Nontenured faculty are now often consulted, but generally do not vote, on merit and promotion recommendations; all tenured faculty increasingly participate in decisions, rather than only those of higher rank than the person under review. Participation in the evaluation process provides junior faculty with increased understanding of, and appreciation for, peer evaluation, while senior faculty may be stimulated and challenged to remain current when their work is subject to review by younger colleagues.

Scarce resources are affecting faculty evaluation by raising standards for promotion to tenure. There is general concurrence that this trend has merit, since standards were probably weakened during the period of rapid expansion. One result is increased turnover at lower levels. This will not necessarily harm an institution unless it results more from unwillingness to commit resources permanently than from applying tough performance standards. Laying off tenured faculty for financial exigency has increased the emphasis on review. Layoffs may be reluctantly accepted when entire programs are eliminated, but laying off individuals within a continuing program for purposes of meeting financial stringencies is being challenged. While evidence for any layoffs must be strong, the record in these latter cases must be adequate to stand potential court scrutiny.

Faculty evaluation must be capable of distinguishing excellent from mediocre performance as a basis for adjusting salaries. With resources scarce, not all faculty members can expect to enjoy regular merit increases and promotions. Faculty evaluation can also assist in improving quality by identifying individuals who are not performing up to their potential and providing guidance for their renewal and revitalization. "Growth contracts" between faculty members and department chairs can help ensure that vitality is retained. These contracts can also help faculty plan their career development, particularly in how they use sabbatical leaves and other opportunities to increase academic strengths and versatility. As colleges and universities increasingly encourage high faculty productivity to compensate for lack of growth, reviewing how faculty members exercise their responsibilities within the considerable freedom they have to set their own goals and priorities can be expected to focus increasingly on these points in assessing individual faculty stewardship.

Aggregate analysis of such faculty characteristics as age, rank, workload, costs, and rate of faculty turnover by department and field provides essential information for planning. If institutional leaders seek greater flexibility in resource use, the proportion of long-term commitments to faculty must be contained or reduced. If they seek academic program change, planned turnover is the most important determinant of when such changes can be instituted. Present evaluation processes can serve all these ends with only minor modifications. This expanded but essential role for faculty evaluation can help colleges and universities retain quality and intellectual vitality despite constraint.

Administrative Performance Review. Presidents, academic vice-presidents, provosts, and deans are usually appointed because of successful faculty service and demonstrated leadership within the academic community. With exceptions, their performance as academic administrators is seldom reviewed regularly after their appointment. Pressures for regular review have risen sharply, particularly from faculty members who are increasingly anxious over administrators' resource and planning decisions. Strong positive arguments exist for reviewing administrative performance in planning, resource management, and assessment; yet a number of factors complicate adoption of formal review procedures.

First, administrators answer to many constituencies—trustees, faculty, students, alumni, funding agencies, donors, and parents—and their performance is subject to review from diverse perspectives and on diverse and not always consistent criteria. Many faculty members believe that their role should be central in the review process, even though faculty do not have authority to appoint administrators, but most governing boards review presidential performance, with no more than advice from faculty or other interested parties.

Second, lack of clear assignment of responsibilities and absence of definitive objectives for administrative performance make the task of review difficult. Multiple reporting lines of academic administrators and their complex relations with governing boards and with faculty in shared governance lead to confusion about criteria for review. One president remarked that his criterion for evaluating deans' performance was whether or not they kept their constituents quiet. Given the inherently controversial choices among programs and resources that administrators will have to make in the future, such a criterion will be less than useful.

Developing criteria in the absence of objectives or goals is futile. Many governing boards fail to develop objectives for the chief executive, and many executives fail to define objectives either for themselves or for their subordinates. Even more rarely do presidents and governing boards jointly set objectives against which administrative performance can be assessed.

More systematic review of academic administrators can improve administrative performance, clarify responsibilities, communicate objectives throughout the institution, and focus administrative decisions on the achievement of objectives. Unlike the work of faculty members, the activities of most administrators can be specified, goals and timetables set, and progress assessed. This distinction is particularly apparent in reviewing the performance of administrative staff and unit managers such as department chairs. Even more than senior administrators, functional managers and staff are assigned clearly defined responsibilities for which specific objectives and measures of performance can be established.

Experience to draw on in suggesting means of conducting necessary reviews is limited. Although evaluation must be unique to the structure of a particular institution, a possible model can be built around the following principles:

- Since the gestation period for accomplishing change in academic programs is long, assessments are best scheduled every three to five years. More frequent reviews are not precluded where specific circumstances may dictate.
- Review should be initiated by the academic administrator to whom the person being reviewed reports. The nature of the process, the type of information to be developed, and the criteria for evaluation should be known both to those being evaluated and to those participating in the review.

- Extensive exchange between the administrator being reviewed and the person or persons to whom he or she reports should be the basis of the review process. A self-analysis of past performance and specific plans for the future can provide a basis for performance review. Information should be sought periodically on the quality of the administrator's stewardship. Faculty, students, alumni, and others with whom the individual works should be consulted. Information sought from each group should be confined, however, to what that group's perspective can lend to the evaluation.
- Although review should focus on performance, it should result in plans for the future. Review should conclude with an agreement, in some instances formally, about objectives for the coming period and perhaps include a planned advancement or broadening of duties. Or it may result in an agreed-on date of resignation, transfer to another assignment, or reduction in responsibility.

A structured process for assessment of academic administrators has clear advantages over the present informal and often unclear procedures. It emphasizes positive accomplishment and improvement rather than negative criticism and helps management bring decisions throughout the organization into concert with planning objectives established by the president, chancellor, or governing board. Forcing a careful, periodic self-assessment of strengths and weaknesses and successes and failures will develop administrators' skills. If proper assessment procedures are in place, administrators can delegate authority, evaluate subordinates' exercise of the delegated authority, and concentrate their own efforts on providing the leadership they are so often criticized for failing to provide.

Assessing Resource Use

Relying on policy guidance and economic incentives rather than central procedural controls requires resource use assessment activities not presently undertaken by most colleges and universities. Assessment of resource use is the primary means by which management retains control under a decentralized mode of operation. To assess resource use means using the results of many types of qualitative and quantitative evaluation. Many measures are available to indicate how effectively and efficiently department chairs and other unit managers use human, financial, physical, and temporal resources to achieve program goals and institutional objectives.

Improving the assessment of resource use solely to meet financial reporting requirements misses an important opportunity for improving resource management: the making of more informed resource use decisions. In multipurpose institutions such as colleges and universities, two efficiency criteria form the basis for the majority of resource decisions: (1) using as few resources as possible to achieve a level of "output" of acceptable quality and (2) for a given level of resources, achieving as large an output as possible, consistent with quality. Minimizing the size of the consulting staff in the computer center while meeting the needs of students and faculty for assistance illustrates the first criterion. Maximizing enrollments in laboratory courses commensurate with the availability of expensive equipment illustrates the second.

Some observers argue that efficiency has been increased in higher education because real resources have been reduced as a result of inflation and tighter budgets. The evidence for this increase is not altogether clear. Across-the-board cuts and salary savings through attrition, often resulting in an inequitable distribution of resources and workload, have been common. Internal planned reallocations directed at maintaining quality and gaining greater efficiency have been uncommon. As emphasized earlier, most academic administrators recognize the shortcomings of their first responses to financial stringencies. Despite limitations on major redistributions, they know that a different distribution of faculty, funds, space, and time could improve overall efficiency within existing resources. Many sense the possibility of improving quality and efficiency by giving subordinates greater discretion in spending these resources. But few have yet been willing to explore the opportunities that remain at the margin for improvement and how improvements can actually be accomplished. Availability of the results of academic, administrative, and personnel program reviews and improved knowledge of resource use can offer the means to this end.

Resource use assessment employs the program resource criteria discussed in Chapter Six, such as student/faculty ratios, class size, and dollars of support per student credit hour, that estimate the resources needed to support a program. These flexible standards may be in physical, monetary, qualitative, or quantitative terms. Certain aspects of present accounting and financial analysis operations can provide some components of the information needed for such assessment; yet the emphasis of accounting on meeting fiduciary responsibility and of budgeting on controlling resource use are not adequate to support resource use assessment. Information that reports actual performance to permit appraisal against program criteria can come from a variety of sources other than traditional accounting and budget systems, including the study of human, space, and time resources through institutional research on faculty workloads, space utilization, time and effort allocations, and other factors.

As noted in Chapter Six, if an institution has established program resource criteria in upper-division biology courses of between 80 and 100 percent in laboratory station use, variation in lecture class size of between seventy and ninety, and variation in instructor classroom contact from seven to ten hours a week, resource use assessment can support resource management in adjusting resource allocations to changing levels of activity and in revising policies by uncovering discrepancies between actual resource use and expected use as put forth in resource plans. If unacceptable discrepancies continue, both program resource criteria and management decisions or expenditures at the operating level must be reviewed. For example, institutional leaders may have determined that three departments have lower than average productivity and that their support dollars are below the minimum acceptable standard. They may have also agreed to increase support dollars in each of the departments over a three-year period to meet the goal of increasing productivity, with authority to allocate dollars to the departments resting with the dean of the college and expenditure authority delegated to the individual department chairs. In most present allocation systems, productivity goals may be set but no new resources provided, or annual support dollars may be line-itemed in a budgeted account to each department but the use to which they are put is probably not questioned. In contrast, program use assessment establishes a method of monitoring support expenditures and productivity in the departments in three years. At the end of the first year, the monitoring procedures indicate that the dean had increased allocations to the three departments equally by 10 percent. Resource use assessment indicates that one department has increased support expenditures a total of 15 percent for teaching equipment and secretarial services by using other funds to augment the 10 percent increase; the second has increased support for teaching materials by only 5 percent, the other 5 percent going for graduate student stipends; the third shows no increase in support expenditures, the entire amount being used for new office furnishings. Only the first two of the three suggest that actions taken may have led to increased productivity. This information alerts the dean to assess these discrepancies in order to determine whether the original planning decision was faulty in some way, whether or not the productivity standards were appropriate, whether needs were properly identified for each department, or whether the second and third chairs merely chose to use the funds for different purposes from those intended. Subsequent action would depend on answers to this inquiry. The dean might, for instance, call the third department's actions into question but leave the added resources in the first two departments, since they achieved the stated goal.

As this illustration shows, monitoring and evaluating resource use can not only trigger resource allocation decisions but also aid the assessment of managerial performance. For example, some department chairs have met budget reductions by reducing secretarial support services below acceptable levels. Faculty members in these departments have had to assume some secretarial duties, and research has been reduced. Rather than responding hastily and perhaps inappropriately to such decisions by partly retracting delegated authority from these chairs, the dean can review the wisdom of such decisions at the time their managerial performance is evaluated and take more considered action.

Past attempts to develop such a capability for resource use assessment by global reform of budgeting and review processes have failed because they imposed too much additional work on too many people. Resource use assessment capability can be established by monitoring and assessing the results of only those selected resource management decisions that are designed to implement a specific intermediate planning goal. It is not necessary to track all decisions in any one year in the same detail. What is necessary initially is to establish a pattern of thinking within the institution about the effective use of resources and ways to assess this use. This approach directs the attention of everyone involved to the new process so that all understand that assessment decisions are to guide future action and that accountability for results is expected. Selection of decisions to be monitored will determine the information requirements of the assessment process, both in terms of that needed by staff for implementation as well as information essential for assessment of results. Information gaps are to be expected in moving to this new resource use assessment approach. But once the approach has been applied selectively, identifying and agreeing on the information essential for assessment at the time resource decisions are made can become an integral part of the decision process.

Reviewing Policy

In Chapter Three we defined policy as the embodiment of institutional objectives and goals in formal statements designed to guide an institution toward achieving those objectives. Good policy is capable of being implemented, monitored for compliance, and assessed for its contribution toward attaining objectives. Through policy review or policy assessment, administrators know the extent to which operational results match institutional objectives and what elements of policy are most effective in achieving those results.

Colleges and universities have bodies of policy dealing with academic programs, personnel practices, financial administration, physical plant, and other areas of institutional operation—from admissions to xerography. The characteristics of good policy apply equally to all areas. Academic policies are typically oriented to the objectives of achieving desired quality and meeting societal needs in teaching and research and are usually stated in general terms. Because of the nature of the academic enterprise and decision mechanisms, such general policy statements work reasonably well, but assessing their effects is difficult and seldom undertaken. Personnel policies are usually more specific than academic policies; yet those designed to deal with current circumstances such as reductions in force and faculty reassignment and retraining are often hastily written in the midst of stressful debate. Policies for financial administration are still primarily oriented to meeting fiduciary responsibilities and the requirements imposed by funding sources. As such, financial "policies" are largely rules and regulations rather than policies as defined earlier, in that they give little attention to whether resources are efficiently used or goals and objectives are effectively met.

In general, college and university policy is less clear than policy in business, government, and most other large organizations. This is not surprising, given the complex objectives and wide range of unmeasurable outcomes in higher education. Yet substantial improvements can be made in increasing clarity by translating broad and general objectives into more specific intermediate goals and these goals into strategies and even more specific policies.

The three examples of typical university objectives, goals, and policies offered in Chapter Three illustrate the importance of assessing policy to ensure that it has the expected consequences. First, sabbatical leave and travel fund policies are common means to the goal of helping faculty members stay at the forefront in their academic disciplines, in order to fulfill the institutional objective of contributing to the advancement of knowledge. Monitoring these policies for compliance with this goal and objective consists in ascertaining which faculty members take leaves or use travel funds, what they do intellectually while on leave or traveling, and whether they make use of these opportunities in their research. Such an analysis quickly reveals whether these programs are used by a small or large part of the faculty, whether participation is skewed by rank, discipline, and type of activity, and whether to approve particular requests for leaves or travel and encourage other faculty members to use the programs. But equally important, by weighing the results of sabbatical leaves and travel against each other and against other policies aimed at aiding faculty research, changes in the policies can be made in order to improve their effectiveness.

Second, achieving excellence in academic programs may require adding new faculty talents even if the size of the faculty remains static. To achieve this flexibility in faculty resources, turnover may need to be increased. To encourage such turnover, some years ago the University of California had promulgated a policy of allocating certain new academic positions on a temporary basis to departments. When this policy was assessed for compliance, university administrators found that departments were indeed making short-term appointments. But when they assessed the policy for results, they learned that these short-term positions were being filled with various kinds of temporary assistants, including students, and that many positions not filled were being cannibalized for support dollars. As a consequence, the university revised this policy to require instead that all departments be prepared to give up 10 percent of their faculty positions on one year's notice. This change shifted departmental emphasis toward more serious long-run planning of the types of faculty resources they required and of the age distribution of the faculty in light of these needs. It also turned out to be an easier policy to monitor for compliance.

To achieve a third common objective of colleges and universities—efficiency in the use of resources—institutions sometimes set a policy of removing all vacated positions from departments for possible reallocation elsewhere. Assessing the results of this policy will ordinarily reveal that departments respond by retaining inferior faculty members who would otherwise be separated in order to retain the position. Such a policy should be modified to exempt positions from being withdrawn that are vacated by reason of adverse personnel actions.

Typically, institutions review their policies on an ad hoc basis when cause for review arises. The lack of routine review of policies is a serious shortcoming of academic administration. Policies may be in force that not only are obsolete but in conflict with institutional goals and objectives. Several methods can ensure policy review, but they have seldom been adapted to the particular needs of colleges and universities. They include canceling each policy at the end of a given period unless reviewed and renewed, reviewing all policies routinely at set intervals, and continuous policy review. The cyclical approach to management advocated in this book triggers continuous review in three ways: (1) through routine audits of policy for compliance with goals and objectives; (2) through issues identified in planning and resource management discussions; and (3) through academic program reviews, administrative and academic support service reviews, and resource use assessments.

Policy reviews can be conducted by members of each operating unit, by a separate administrative unit reporting to the chief executive officer, or by special task forces consisting of unit members and administrative staff. Each approach has advantages and disadvantages. Self-evaluation by unit members has the advantage that these members learn from the review about the effectiveness of the policies they have implemented, and they are directly responsible for increasing the effectiveness of their unit. For these reasons many believe that self-evaluation should be a major goal of academic administration and of education at large (Hodgkinson and others, 1975). Self-evaluation suffers, however, from the danger of parochialism, partiality, and lack of objectivity. But when evaluation activities are separated from operating units and conducted by administrative staff alone, the gains in objectivity may be offset by a lack of intimate knowledge of the unit.

Our experience indicates that it is best to balance these strengths and weaknesses by including in a task force both unit members affected by the policy and people from outside the unit who have a range of skills appropriate to studying the policy. For example, the analysis of financial aid policies could include a senior administrative officer in the financial aid area, a financial aid staff member responsible for helping units interpret policy, an accountant, a recipient of financial aid, an information systems specialist, and a staff analyst who could coordinate the review, bring the perspective and concern of central administrators into the review process, and help obtain consistency between the financial aid policies and other policies. The recommendations developed by such a "cross-functional" task force are sensitive to a wide variety of policy concerns. Equally important, such task forces have the added benefit, over time, of making many people capable of reviewing policy—a talent they can carry into their own jobs and their own self-assessment.

Conclusion

It is impossible to think of planning and resource management apart from assessment. Without assessment, planning is quite sterile and resource management inadequately targeted. Assessment of the results of past actions produces the information that administrators need to judge the consistency of resource decisions with plans. It provides insight into whether the mechanisms they are using are effective and efficient, and it serves as a guide for further refinement of plans and policies.

Like all professionals who believe that their own internal standards of performance are adequate and that self-assessment should be sufficient, professors have a historical reluctance toward any kind of management oversight. Their concern has increased as academic administrators have failed to explain the reasons for oversight, define the unique roles of faculty and administration in the assessment process, or specify how the results of assessment will be used. Some administrative oversight has been rightly criticized for its lack of sophistication in introducing assessment techniques into the university environment from other institutions without sufficient modification. Failure to adopt modern management procedures reflects a lack of experience on the part of many academic administrators with management concepts essential to effective operation of today's large and complex academic institutions.

Overcoming faculty concern and other obstacles to more systematic assessment will be one of the most difficult management tasks of the remainder of the 1980s. The fact that academic program review is evolving from the sound foundation of faculty peer review, with reviewers drawn from both inside and outside the programs under review, augurs well for faculty acceptance of more systematic review of other facets of institutional operation—but only if administrators fulfill their responsibility for oversight by involving faculty and staff in the assessment process. Information gathered cooperatively in assessment processes can more adequately capture the complexities of university operations and contribute to better performance than that sought unilaterally by administrators or demanded by external agencies. It can lead to decentralized management where traditional precontrols by external agencies, central administrators, and bureaucratic staff give way in large measure to postperformance review of the results of units' own decisions. By leading to improved planning and resource management at all levels of the institution, assessment completes and renews the management cycle.

9

Applying Techniques for Evaluating Programs, Personnel, and Resource Use

All colleges and universities conduct each of the five types of performance assessment discussed in Chapter Eight —reviews of academic programs, administrative and academic support services, personnel, resource use, and policy. The methods, the information developed, and the effectiveness with which it is used vary widely from institution to institution. This chapter illustrates how the University of California has used each of the five types of assessment. It emphasizes the reasons for specific assessments, their objectives, the problems encountered in their conduct, and their results. The chapter illustrates how assessment can aid planning and resource management.

Academic Program Review

The University of California relies heavily on faculty initiative and participation for the review of academic programs.

165

Faculty on all campuses regularly review courses and degree programs. In recent years, as resource constraints have led to more and more difficult program choices, the orientation of these campus initiated reviews has shifted from the quality of program plans to the relation among existing programs both on a given campus and between campuses, as well as their conformity with institutional mission and scope. As noted in Chapter Eight, these expanded objectives of program review are increasingly necessary, but they give rise to new controversy among departments, between the faculty and administration, and among campuses in the system.

Besides campus-initiated program reviews, the university periodically undertakes systemwide reviews. Five such cross-campus reviews from the 1970s illustrate the variety possible in the objectives, approaches, outcomes, and effectiveness of program reviews in guiding academic change.

Matching Program Demand and Capacity: Engineering. Along with the basic sciences, engineering was an important component of the university's growth in the 1950s and 1960s. New engineering schools or programs were developed on three of the nine campuses, and initial commitments, including the appointment of a dean, were made for a fourth. Given the cost of such programs, however, and the fact that the rapidly expanding California State University and College System was also developing new engineering schools, University of California officials launched a review of engineering offerings within the university before the fourth program materialized. A team composed of faculty members and industry leaders undertook an exhaustive study of the expected demand for, and developing supply of, engineers in California with special reference to the university's plans.

The result of the review was that the incipient program was terminated. The decision was not popular on the campus, but slow growth rates in several of the university's other engineering programs over the next several years appeared to support it. Since then, however, continued technological growth has pushed quality engineering programs to the limit of their enrollment, with demand still outpacing supply. Given the cyclic job market in engineering, the decision not to develop a fourth program would most likely have been different had the review occurred several years later. At the time, however, the decision was not unwarranted, taking into account current projections.

Assuring Program Quality Along with Capacity: Administrative Science. Similar and additional concerns prompted a systemwide review of all business and public administration teaching and research programs in the university. Two campuses had made strong cases for launching new programs in administration, while questions had surfaced about the quality of several new, small programs on other campuses that had not yet undergone any review. For this study, the review team consisted of faculty members drawn from the several campuses and leaders of business and industry, with staff support provided by the central office. The team carefully reviewed and evaluated the existing and planned programs, examining their objectives, capacity, quality, and plans for development. It then made extensive suggestions for strengthening the academic content of two existing programs and sharpening the objectives of at least one other program. It also recommended that the two planned programs (one of which had already been approved) not be developed. The recommendations were implemented, canceling one of the two planned programs and postponing development of the other for approximately five years until student demand grew sufficiently strong and resources could be identified to assure an adequate program.

Reviewing Program Expansion and Interinstitutional Relations: Marine Sciences. Proposals for expanding two small research and instruction programs in marine sciences triggered a review of all marine sciences programs currently available in the University of California, considering as well those offered by other institutions in the state. Expanding the two programs would have required extensive investment, and the already world-renowned Scripps Institution of Oceanography on the university's San Diego campus would continue to require more resources in order to retain its preeminence.

The charge to the review team developed by the Academic Planning and Program Review Board called for a definition of the objectives, scope, and plans for each of the university's programs plus an assessment of offerings of other institutions and the implications of further development of marine sciences for the university campuses involved as well as for the total university system. The review team of scientists, with systemwide staff assistance, assembled and evaluated extensive material and interviewed university and outside scholars; yet its report was of little use in guiding future decisions. Its recommendations tended to concentrate on minor aspects of the programs; it avoided the politically sensitive interinstitutional issues and offered little guidance for future resource commitments. In retrospect, its inadequacies were less the fault of the review team than of the review process. The diversity of the several marine sciences programs was too great for a modest review, despite the competence of the team members. The objectives of the assessment and the definition of the units included in the charge was overly inclusive, with departments, research laboratories, contract operations, land-based facilities, and research vessels all among the units that could be encompassed.

Nonetheless, over time the report did assist in strengthening the university's marine sciences offerings. It alerted systemwide administrators to related resources and facilities on several campuses that could be used in the programs. In addition, the review process itself encouraged the personnel in each unit to articulate the unit's role and aspirations; it increased the visibility of the units—until then, largely unknown even on their own campuses; and provided information to counter concern of the California Postsecondary Education Commission about excessive overlap and redundancy among the programs.

Defining the University's Role: Teacher Education. Declining school enrollments, the existence of extensive teacher training programs outside the university, and the substantial resources committed to teacher training on several of its campuses raised questions about the role of the university in "professional" education—a field long suspect among arts and science faculty.

Great care was taken in this review to develop an appropriate charge by widely circulating drafts of the charge to faculty committees and administrators for comments and suggestions before putting it in final form. A distinguished faculty member with extensive administrative experience agreed to chair the review team, and the state superintendent of public instruction served as an active member.

After a year of intensive study, the team articulated a clear three-part role for university programs in education: (1) to set standards for primary and secondary institutions; (2) to experiment and innovate with new instructional approaches; and (3) to expand and upgrade the quality of research on teaching and learning processes. The team was critical of vestiges of traditional "teacher training" activities and called on the university administration and faculty to give existing programs a new direction.

Some improvements resulted from this far-reaching review, but needed changes in teacher training were slow to materialize. Careful assessment and thoughtful recommendations did not guarantee rapid improvement, for the faculty members on whom change ultimately depended were unable to implement the recommendations. Major change had to wait for either extensive retraining and turnover of the teacher education faculty or assumption of responsibility for the change by administrators and faculty bodies at a higher level where other incentives could be brought to bear on the education faculty.

Intercampus Cooperation: Classics. On any campus offering doctoral programs, professors aspire to participate in such programs, preferably designed and controlled by their own department. Such aspirations are a significant indicator of a quality faculty, but not every discipline and subdiscipline can be offered effectively at the doctoral level on all campuses. The role of program review in dealing with this issue was exemplified at the University of California by the development of graduate programs in classics at two campuses beyond Berkeley and UCLA, which already offered the Ph.D. degree in classics and had the necessary library collections, laboratory facilities, and museum holdings to support programs of high quality. Irvine, one of the new campuses of the university, originally developed its small classics Ph.D. program as a "satellite" of the UCLA program. Another smaller campus had a highly successful undergraduate offering in classics, and its vigorous faculty had been pressing for a Ph.D. program. Clearly, review of classics graduate offerings in the university was called for.

A review team consisting of scholars from the university and other nationally recognized programs was asked to assess the quality of the existing programs, the need for developing any new programs, and the potential of the interested campus and its faculty to offer a high-quality program should the need be substantiated.

The review team cited the strengths of the existing program on one of the two large campuses and pointed out a number of ways the program on the other large campus could be improved. It commended the university for its intercampus sharing of faculty and other resources in the interest of program strength and efficiency, as illustrated by the Irvine/UCLA cooperation. It complimented the strength and quality of the faculty seeking approval for the other new doctoral program but recommended against establishing the program on the ground that the need could be met elsewhere in the system.

The president sought a compromise about the new program. He suggested that the satellite concept be expanded to include it. This avoided the investment in library and other resources that would be required for a completely independent new program while allowing its faculty to participate in an existing program and strengthening the existing program with the infusion of new academic blood. The final outcome was the development of a separate master's degree program rather than a doctoral program on the small campus.

These five examples point out several common facets of academic program review. First, each review presents at least one unique problem or issue that needs to be taken into account in wording its charge, selecting review team members, conducting the review, and drafting its report.

Second, program reviews such as these are costly, both in time and in money. Unless they are used to bring about improvement, they are not cost-effective. Therefore, experience suggests that they should be undertaken selectively and for specific purposes. It is tempting to schedule academic program reviews as a quality control device on a regular basis, but the superficiality associated with routine reviews not only is costly but defeats many of the purposes of assessment.

Third, even with the greatest care and diligence in reviewing programs, limits exist about what can be accomplished in the short run, given political and economic realities. Implementation takes time; academic program reviews do not in themselves accomplish change. They are merely one tool for change in the hands of policy makers, one that is often more powerful over the long-run than in the short run.

Administrative and Academic Support Services Review

Within the University of California, each campus periodically reviews its administrative and academic support services to ensure that they meet current needs and their assigned responsibilities effectively and efficiently. Because these reviews are frequent and thus expected, and because they stem from campus self-assessment and are conducted largely by the campus administration, they are not particularly threatening to the persons involved. A different situation confronted systemwide administration in the middle 1970s. Over two decades, as the individual campuses of the university had grown in size and stature, the university had evolved from a system with two "flagship" campuses, the president administering the entire system, toward a more decentralized organization. As the task of managing the university centrally grew increasingly difficult, authority for managing certain administrative activities on the various campuses was delegated to the local campus chancellors. Successive presidents had been urged to adopt an even more decentralized administrative structure by shifting the role of the president's office further from the management of campus operations to policy making and control through planning, resource management, and assessment. The longstanding challenge by the campuses to the continued role of systemwide officers in administering campus activities continued into the 1970s. Questions about specific administrative functions were raised not only by the campus chancellors but by executive and legislative officials in state government and by the university's external auditors. Some needed reorganization was accomplished and preliminary clarification of roles was attempted in the 1960s and early 1970s, but the change in administration in 1975 provided a new opportunity for examining and altering some longstanding administrative structures and relationships. Six examples of administrative and academic support services reviews during the 1970s illustrate the issues that confronted the systemwide administration.

Updating Administrative Services: Systemwide Organization and Operations. President Saxon immediately reduced the number of senior systemwide administrators in order to adapt the systemwide administrative structure to his leadership style. He appointed three remaining senior vice-presidents to assist him in reviewing systemwide administration. He also established a task force on the Systemwide Administration of the University of California, consisting of faculty and staff from campuses as well as from systemwide offices. His initial charge to the task force asked it to assess the need for change in the nature, location, direction, and priorities of systemwide administrative activities and how central policy formulation could be improved and its impact better assessed. Subsequently, he broadened this charge to include how planning and resource management could be better integrated and how the interaction between the systemwide offices and the campuses could be made more effective and efficient.

The task force wisely focused its attention on defining principles and concepts that could guide later reviews of individual offices and operations rather than undertaking the monumental and probably impossible task of assessing each unit in detail. By so doing, its report (University of California, 1977a) was able to emphasize the importance of improving the leadership of the systemwide administration in policy formulation, policy review, and external relations through academic planning and resource management. It endorsed further delegation of operational authority and responsibility to the campuses, and suggested reorganization of the systemwide offices and staff.

This latter recommendation included a call for an administrative plan that would reduce the numbers of management and professional staff and would introduce improved communication within and among the systemwide offices. Indirectly these recommendations sought to break down the last vestiges of the "baronies" remaining from the era of centralized operations, to reduce internal formality and paper shuffling, and to fix responsibility for decisions while forcing cross-functional interaction among administrators in reaching these decisions.

The report of the task force resulted in some initial reorganization and consolidation of responsibilities under the vice-presidents. It also induced a number of additional assessments of specific functions, some of which are discussed below. But cooperation was difficult to obtain from those who believed their power might be lessened or were fearful for their position. The senior administrators to whom fell the task of achieving the reorganization were not experienced in managing conflict and change, and they found that their ongoing responsibilities demanded a full measure of their time. Despite this slow progress, the many persons at all levels who were interviewed during the review gained new insights into their own jobs; campus leaders saw their administrative needs more clearly than before and took steps to strengthen their administrative operations; and a framework was created for more detailed reviews of specific offices and functions.

Moving from Operations to Policy: Business Affairs. The presidential task force review of systemwide administration led directly to a review of business affairs. Eight staff members from the campuses and systemwide administration were assembled to (1) identify policy-related business affairs functions, as opposed to those that were operational, (2) suggest a realignment of functions to keep policy at the systemwide level and move operations to the campuses, (3) recommend organizational structure, staffing, policies, and procedures for carrying out the systemwide functions more effectively, and (4) provide a plan to implement these changes. The review team found that many business affairs functions were already duplicated on campuses and at the systemwide level, except on some of the smaller campuses. Thus, overall staff reductions would be possible by transferring a number of these operational functions entirely to the campuses. The team also recommended several organizational realignments and staffing changes at the systemwide level, some of which required further study before implementation could be undertaken.

Even before the team formally submitted its report, some of its recommendations were being implemented. Possible self-insurance by the university rather than continued heavy reliance on centrally purchased insurance was immediately explored, since there was reason to believe that self-insurance could achieve substantial savings. The business staff was reduced slightly, and some positions at the supervisory level were reassigned. But again, implementation was less than it might have been. Inexperienced administrators, internal staff resistance, and reluctance to face the trauma of change impeded full reform.

Moving Beyond Data to Information: Administrative Information Systems. After the university's first comprehensive study of financial, student, personnel, and logistical information systems in 1965-66, the president's office created an Information Systems Division to develop three major administrative information systems: Accounting, Student and Personnel, and Advanced Models and Simulation. The task was arduous and not well executed, inviting periodic criticism from external auditors and the legislature and a number of successful attempts by individual campuses to develop their own separate and usually incompatible systems. Despite the policy of systemwide administration to restrict administrative computing to two locations in the state, the availability of less and less expensive computers invited its violation by the campuses. Complicating the problem was the temptation to defray equipment costs by conducting administrative computing on computers obtained for research and instruction purposes. General frustration over the mounting financial commitment—amounting to millions of dollars—and recurring disappointment with the resulting data led to another review in 1975. A broadly based task force of faculty and campus and systemwide administrative staff was appointed to review the status of the university's information systems and recommend improvements in them. Its report (University of California, 1976) contained realistic and practical recommendations for decentralizing information system development to the campuses where capability had been demonstrated in specific areas such as accounting and student records. But common definitions of basic data elements were to be developed so that comparative analyses across campuses would be possible. Control over financial information was to remain with the systemwide administration in order to meet its corporate fiduciary responsibilities.

The report generated extensive debate over reallocation of funds and personnel between the systemwide administration and the campuses, over appropriate aggregation and disclosure of data at various levels, and over continuation of the all-inclusive integrated systems approach as opposed to a variety of restricted-purpose systems. Had this review followed that of the systemwide administration, it might have been more productive, since the clarification of organizational and operational issues would have made the task of defining information needs much easier. As it was, however, much was learned from this review of information systems that facilitated the later review of systemwide administration.

Adjusting Staffing to Changed Needs: Architects and Engineers. During the 1950s and 1960s, planning, designing, and constructing university facilities to meet growing enrollments and expanding research and service activities required an extensive staff of professional architects and engineers. The university was particularly successful in assembling a high-quality staff at both the systemwide and campus levels that met the challenges of growth successfully. With the decline in growth rate and reduced construction budgets, the activities of this staff shifted toward remodeling and preventive maintenance. Questions arose about the size and skills of the staff, both within the university and in the legislature. A few staff positions were removed by the legislature, but serious cuts were deferred pending further analysis.

Given the sensitivity of the issue and the technical nature of the required assessment, the university hired both a management consulting firm and an engineering consulting firm to jointly assess the present and future needs for skills in this area, how they should be distributed within the university and its campuses, and what organizational structure and policies would best serve the university's needs in the period ahead. The consultants developed a working technical committee within the university to assist in their deliberations.

The consultants' report provided excellent guidance on needed staffing levels and desirable distribution of talents among campus and systemwide offices. It also offered specific suggestions on how the architectural and engineering activities could be better coordinated with other planning and management functions of the university. The report recommended overall reduction of the staff and redistribution of resources to the campuses to meet local architectural and engineering needs associated with remodeling, overcoming local and state code deficiencies, and conserving energy. And it recommended strengthening systemwide relations with state agencies and ensuring systemwide compliance with various quality control policies and regulations.

This assessment provided the necessary guidance for staffing changes. It also lessened legislative pressure to make indiscriminate reductions in the university's budget, since the university was demonstrably addressing the problem over a reasonable period of time.

Improving Staff Skills: Budgetary Planning and Operations. From the early 1970s, more effort was spent over a longer period of time in assessing resource planning and allocation than in any other single assessment activity at the systemwide level. Early in the decade, a task force of senior staff and administrators was instructed to develop a planning-operating concept of budgeting and accounting. This group concluded that significant changes would be needed in organization, procedures, and human skills if the university were to integrate planning and resource management adequately. Subsequent analyses by systemwide staff and administrators over several years examined existing staff activities to discover how budgeting might be better integrated with other, related administrative functions. Allocation actions to campuses were monitored to see whether they were consistent with policy decisions. This analysis uncovered the problems of multiple allocations at various times during the year and the excessive contraints imposed by central resource control discussed in Chapter Seven.

Several improvements were made, including greater interaction with the regents in preparing their annual budget request to the legislature and the governor, earlier development of campus resource needs, and streamlining the allocation of resources to campuses. High priority was assigned to separating the political and tactical aspects of acquiring state funds from the internal criteria and processes for allocating these funds and to placing greater emphasis on resource planning and assessment of actual resource use and less on review of transactions.

The two reviews of administrative information systems and of systemwide administration that were discussed earlier verified many of these problems and conclusions. They also identified overlapping and unclear budgetary responsibilities between offices, poor communication of planning decisions and options to resource planners, and an overemphasis on formality and bureaucracy in budget activities. These problems characterized a centralized precontrol orientation as opposed to a resource planning and objective-oriented postcontrol philosophy. The two studies suggested additional changes in organization and assignment of responsibilities that would increase the responsiveness of the resource management function to planning objectives. Taken as a group, all three studies pointed to ways of reducing the size of the budget staff while increasing its capability and effectiveness.

An evaluation of staff in budget and financial operations pointed to the desirability of transferring some employees into more responsible positions where they could make a greater contribution, of terminating others, and of broadening the experience of the rest. A limited number of systemwide budget staff members were therefore temporarily assigned to the campuses to gain greater familiarity with administration at the operating level. Others were assigned to various task forces to gain broader perspective on pressing resource issues. These short-term assignments helped determine which individuals could most likely contribute to the new mode of resource management toward which the university was moving. All in all, this series of assessment activities involving budgeting significantly facilitated the extensive changes in planning and resource management within the university that were described in Chapters Four and Seven.

Upgrading Academic Support Services: Libraries. A series of reviews of various aspects of library development and operation conducted over nearly a decade illustrates the value of continued assessment as a means of reaching workable and acceptable solutions to complex and controversial issues central to the quality of academic institutions. Assessment of all aspects of library activities and needs was both encouraged and complicated by the rapidly rising costs of procuring, processing, storing, and managing the use of library materials. Even though enrollment and physical plant growth tapered off, the growth of new knowledge and costs associated with it continued unabated. Concern over rising costs had led the California Department of Finance to an independent study that added impetus to the planning of internal assessments.

The first of several internal studies dealt primarily with acquisition rates and the geographic location of library collections for the system. A second study focused on providing adequate storage space in relation to known and expected technology. By 1974, the reactions and counterreactions to these earlier studies had increased the understanding of the broader policy needs in future library development. But one more presidential task force—a Steering Committee for Systemwide Library Policy Implementation—was needed to build support for new library planning policies. An executive director of university-wide library planning was appointed to resolve remaining planning and policy issues. These assessment and planning activities eventually resulted in a comprehensive plan that has effectively guided subsequent library development (University of California, 1977b).

In summary, reviews of administrative and academic support services have many of the same problems as academic program reviews. They are often costly to conduct, in both time and money. Implementing recommendations is always difficult. Skill in human relations is essential to bringing about change with a minimum of anxiety and disruption—an attribute too many managers possess in short supply. In addition, the reports typically do not contain the level of detail that unit managers would like; yet responsibility for implementation must be the manager's.

Two lessons from the experience of the University of California may help make such reviews more effective. First, using respected and experienced faculty members on the assessment team introduces a "user perspective" to the evaluation of administrative and academic support activities not likely to be considered adequately if reviews are conducted only by staff and administrators. Outside consultants can likewise be of particular value when the subject matter is highly technical and when the internal controversy likely to follow recommendations for change is expected to be high.

Second, an initial broad assessment followed by more detailed analyses can improve the quality of reviews as well as educate affected constituencies. The education of constituents takes time, and careful reviews, even if they must be conducted more than once, can gain an acceptable level of concurrence for appropriate actions.

Personnel Performance Review

Faculty Review. The University of California has a long history of reviewing faculty performance. Confidential evaluations by peers and a highly formal process result in recommendations that are followed except in an extremely small percentage of cases in which the campus chancellor or academic vice-chancellor chooses to act counter to faculty advice. On some campuses some actions are delegated to college deans. The person being reviewed is consulted in assembling the supporting documentation and is informed of the recommendation being made by his or her department, including the unidentified vote count of the person's colleagues.

Ad hoc review committees are appointed in the case of all

major proposed actions such as promotion to evaluate documents concerning quality and extent of teaching, research, other creative and scholarly activities, and of other forms of service for the public and the university. Membership on these committees is not revealed to the candidate or to the department. The evaluation and recommendation are then reviewed by a college or campus personnel committee (depending on the level of action), and a recommendation is made to the administration. The findings and recommendations are made known to the individual as a means of improving faculty performance over time and to allow for possible challenge should the individual feel his or her record was improperly evaluated.

Although the process requires significant faculty time, it has proved to be eminently fair and successful in channeling rewards to those whose performance so warrants. It has established known standards of quality of performance to which all faculty members are expected to adhere. The process has shown a remarkable ability to reflect changing values through time, as illustrated by the increased emphasis placed on quality of undergraduate teaching performance since the late 1960s.

Administrator Review. Management and staff personnel review has not developed in a parallel manner to that for faculty. More progress should have been made in objective forms of performance review for management and staff. Salary adjustments and promotions are merit-based, but how merit is established and the criteria for decisions by supervisors are not as clear as they might be. The existence of separate faculty and management/staff evaluation processes in the same organization is occasionally the source of minor misunderstanding and friction between persons in the two groups, particularly when the salary levels and financial rewards at any one time happen to be compared. Such misunderstanding is to be expected, given the disparate responsibilities between faculty members and managers and staff. Greater sophistication in review of managers and staff could alleviate some of the tension.

The University of California has established formal performance review processes for departmental chairs, for deans, and more recently for chancellors. While the procedures are reasonably well established, the variation in quality of review is probably greater than in faculty review, reflecting the greater difficulty in judging performance in assignments where the numbers are fewer and those experienced to judge stewardship less numerous. Also interpersonal political stresses arise, for evaluated administrators are viewed as being in positions to exercise control in the future.

In sum, faculty performance review in the University of California is a model of quality control through assessment and incentives for improvement of performance. While the processes must differ, the same effectiveness should be sought in assessing management and staff performance, particularly if an institution embarks on the integrated management approach advocated in this book.

Resource Use Review

Assessment of faculty workloads and turnover, reflecting a concern for overall productivity, renewal rates, and future resource demands for faculty, is the most common example of resource use reviews in the University of California, as elsewhere. External questions regarding the numbers of courses and students taught by faculty in various ranks have led to administrative attempts to measure teaching "workload" first by sample survey techniques and later by computer-based information systems. Definitional and reporting problems were difficult to overcome, and the results were not acceptable to the faculty. Subsequently, the faculty contracted privately for a similar annual analysis. The results from all the approaches have been numerically similar and have fueled a continuing discussion of the appropriate division of faculty time among an array of partly competing responsibilities. Campuses have become increasingly involved in assessing turnover rates in individual departments and colleges in order to plan for reallocation and renewal as growth slows. The systemwide offices assess turnover rates by campus to gain insight into overall renewal capability, future salary needs, and operating policies at the campus level on rate of advancement and retention rates.

Other than such faculty resource studies and an occasional in-depth analysis of a specific resource use question such as financial aid recipients and space requirements or use, resource use assessment at the systemwide level of the university has been confined historically to reviewing budget-to-budget changes and comparing campus-to-campus budgeted levels by expenditure category. During a growth era these forms of assessment were only minimally adequate, for they overlooked such important aspects as unbudgeted midyear supplements, internal transfers between budgeted categories after initial allocations were made, and other resources expended in activities that were not budgeted. Since a premium was placed on minimizing apparent differences between state-approved budgets and actual expenditures, end-of-year reconciliations rendered year-to-year budget comparisons largely fruitless, as actual expenditures increasingly departed from budgets. Normal assessment processes were unable to provide adequate data to support reallocation plans or assess financial performance of operating units.

In assessing internal budget processes, financial information systems, and accounting practices in the middle 1970s, a number of needed changes were immediately obvious. A tighter link between budget activity and accounting was essential if differences between true expenditures and budgets were to be discernible. The accounting system had to be altered from a strictly fund accounting system to one that matched accounts to programs or activities to be assessed. This meant that a new chart of accounts was required.

Early efforts to improve resource assessment and management capabilities included an attempt to cross over from the traditional object-class, or functional, budget to a program budget. Except for a few persons directly involved, this exercise contributed little to the understanding of what was needed to improve assessment capability.

The information systems task force mentioned earlier pinpointed the deficiencies in defining financial information needs for management and particularly the insufficient appreciation of the usefulness of accurate expenditure data in planning of all types. A task force was created to plan corrective action, but three additional problems were encountered: (1) those appointed to it were not sufficiently close to decision makers to carry out the assigned task; (2) those who were trying to re-design the financial information systems were not managers and were not adequately guided by them; and (3) the task force immediately confronted the fact that delineation between system-wide and campus responsibilities for information needed in corporate decision making was so unclear that further progress was not possible until this issue was resolved. Personalities and institutional politics further exacerbated what was already a most difficult assessment problem.

A senior budget officer was relieved from operating responsibilities for one year to design an approach to resource use assessment consistent with the principles of resource management outlined in Chapter Six. In carrying out this responsibility, a steering group composed of faculty members from the university's two major business schools and one of the schools of public policy was assembled. The budget officer sought to determine information needed to evaluate the results of the multiyear resource decisions discussed in Chapter Seven. It was found that the decisions lent themselves to evaluation, in that the goals and policies were sufficiently specific to apply qualitative and quantitative measurements. It was necessary, however, to interpret and clarify almost all budgetary decisions before they could be adequately implemented and assessed, since even with the best of intentions and care, units had a difficult time understanding specific terms and policies—such as what constituted a "guaranteed base budget" or the implications of a 10 percent flexibility policy regarding faculty positions. Information gaps were to be expected in moving to a new approach. To specify the criteria and the content of the information essential for resource use assessment, the format illustrated in Tables 3 and 4 was tested to summarize and translate each multiyear resource decision at the time the decision was made. To ensure that the evaluation would serve its intended purposes, the eight elements of the decision summary were defined as follows:

• *Action Item:* A precise statement of each resource allocation decision for which tracking and assessment are considered desirable.

Table 3. Sample Decision Summary.

Action Item:	Resource allocations for the two-year period 19__-__ to 19__-__ include additional flexibility for the campus in the use of funds and provide additional instructional resources for teaching assistants, instructional support, and equipment replacement.
Reference:	Letter, vice-president to chancellor, April 29, 19__.
Policy:	We are attempting, in our resource management, to recognize campus needs for instructional support to help make better use of current faculty resources and to help campuses effect internal changes by increasing flexibility.
Purpose or Goal:	It is our expectation that with policy changes to increase campus flexibility in managing resources, provision of additional teaching assistants, and increased funding for instructional supporting programs, the campus will be better able to plan and use more effectively its present resources to further enhance quality.
	Getting the most from existing faculty positions in their teaching role also depends on adequate instructional support. We hope that the increased general instructional support (\$____ in 19__-__ and another \$____ in 19__-__) will allow the campus to use more effectively the relatively large number of unfilled faculty provisions the campus currently has.
Conditions:	None specified.
Commitment for Future Action:	Campus will be expected to fill currently unfilled faculty provisions by the end of the planning period.
Criteria for Evaluation:	Additional flexibility and resources should enable the campus to accommodate its highest-priority needs in the instructional area and to reduce the number of unfilled faculty positions.
Information Required, Including Source and Timing:	Campuses should report on actions taken to date with respect to the use of budgeted faculty positions. The campus should also clarify plans for resolution of problem areas. The campus should identify approaches to adapt present policy and budget procedures to enhance the campus's ability to generate internal flexibility.

- *Reference:* Specific identification of formal communication(s) that sets forth the resource decision.
- *Policy:* The principle or principles on which the resource decision is based, giving recognition to both the ends to be achieved and the means used to arrive at them. In the con-

Table 4. Sample Decision Summary.

Action Item:	By June 30, 19___, the campus must have the capability to provide _____full-time equivalent (FTE) instructional positions to Systemwide on a minimum of one year's notice.
Reference:	Letter, vice-president to chancellor, April 29, 19___.
Policy:	We are imposing a policy on all campuses that requires each campus to manage so that 10 percent of its total instructional FTE faculty can be available to Systemwide on a minimum of one year's notice.
Purpose or Goal:	We believe that campus-level flexibility is critically important in the use of faculty and instructional resources. We have a responsibility to assure that a certain level of flexibility exists within the system so that changes, if they do become necessary, can be made with a minimum of disruption.
Conditions:	Capability must be in place by June 30, 19___.
Commitment for Future Action:	We do not have reason to believe that it will be necessary to recall such positions in the foreseeable future.
Criteria for Evaluation:	Campus should be able to demonstrate that the positions in question are distributed such that the loss of the positions would still permit the campus to cover necessary and ongoing workload. There should be evidence that the campus has established a means to return positions, if called upon to do so. Campus should be able to explain the effects on campus programs if such positions would be lost, and to demonstrate that loss of such positions would not violate current personnel policies.
Information Required, Including Source and Timing:	Narrative explanation by the campus of action taken to date and explanation of the effects of the action taken on meeting departmental workload and on accommodation of university personnel policy. Report should be submitted in September of each year to take advantage of actual year data and coming year budget data.

text of resource evaluation, policy is defined as a principle, plan, or course of action set forth by the president or the vice-president of the university.

- *Purpose or Goal:* The intended aim or effect of the policy on which the resource decision is based; also, clarification, if necessary, of the relationship between the resource decision and the underlying policy.

- *Conditions:* Any stipulations or requisites identified as necessary for occurrence of the designated action; any prerequisites or set of terms established or actions considered essential to fulfillment of the action item.
- *Commitment for Future Action:* Any agreement to do something germane to the action item that is not included in the action item at this time.
- *Criteria for Evaluation:* Identification of means to judge the success of the designated action or to measure the value of the action; identification of principles or facts that will permit results to be compared and judgments formed.
- *Information Required, Including Source and Timing:* Identification of formal evaluation requirements, including who will do the evaluation, types of information required, and timing. Evaluation activity includes gathering a body of facts and setting forth ideas inferred from these facts. When appropriate, the evaluation should also describe conditions that have caused modification or restriction of the intended action.

Policy Review

In practice, policy review is probably the most difficult type of assessment to institute. Writing, editing, and achieving clarity in policy statements are not the problems, though much staff attention goes to these aspects of policy. The real challenge is to ferret out inconsistencies between policies, to update them to ensure that they further institutional objectives and program goals, and to keep detailed procedures from superseding them. In the University of California, as in most other colleges and universities, all these shortcomings could be identified in various policies. The complex nature of the university almost guarantees some inadvertent inconsistency and contradiction among policies, but because of the historical independence between functional offices, the extent of these inconsistencies and contradictions was cause for concern in the middle 1970s.

The task of reviewing all systemwide policy was obviously too great to undertake at one time. Alternatively, those areas of policy most critical to improving resource use were selected for assessment, since developing multiyear resource allocation for greater campus flexibility was the major objective at the time. Over an eight-month period, a fund-use task force composed of systemwide budget, accounting, resource policy, and business services staff members studied all university policies relevant to fund use. Among its major accomplishments, this task force (1) determined the existing legal and historical constraints on the use of all funds and the flexibility that existed to change these constraints; (2) estimated the long-run viability and future income of various funds on the basis of alternative assumptions about key variables; (3) identified opportunities to change policy on individual fund use to facilitate redirecting resources to more nearly meet present and future objectives; (4) attempted to develop a means of tracking fund availability, commitments to campuses involving future liens on funds, and potential unfunded needs that could require support; and (5) assessed possible changes in public policy that could affect either state or federal support and estimated impacts of these changes under varying assumptions about direction, magnitude, and timing.

As a result of its assessment, the task force recommended fundamental changes in the use of several major university fund sources, including the University Opportunity Fund, described in Chapter Seven. Information developed by the task force also allowed inaugurating the multiyear funding program and establishing reserve levels to meet unforeseen shortfalls and opportunities. With greater ability to review past expenditures, university administrators could improve the quality of their projections of future needs and could link potential program changes to resource implications. Most important, from a policy perspective this assessment allowed administrators to set new policies for use of funds at the operating level and to reduce preexpenditure control.

This review of the use of funds was one of the most effective means of educating staff and managers about resource issues and problems and, particularly, of imparting better understanding of the university's changing approach to planning and resource management. At the same time, it helped pinpoint the real information needs of administrators at various levels.

Like academic program and administrative service reviews, each policy review is different, requiring unique skills, different timetables, and carefully drawn charges. To assure the consistency of policy review with other planning, resource management, and assessment activities requires special coordination from high administrative levels.

Conclusion

The experience of the University of California with these different approaches to assessment leads to five generalizations.

First, the techniques of assessment should reflect the nature of the institution, its administrative and academic organization, its governance structures, its delegations of authority and responsibility, and the quality of its leadership. For example, on mature campuses with long experience in internal self-study and a confident faculty and administration, assessment can be undertaken with little formality or outside assistance. In contrast, other campuses may need to rely heavily on outside consultants as reviewers and evaluators. On some campuses, administrators may have to provide extensive guidance in academic program review, while on others the faculty may be experienced as well as willing and able to take major responsibility for it.

Second, every review, even if informal, must be carefully planned and executed if wise courses of action are to follow from it. Those who initiate assessments must think hard about appropriate objectives, criteria, guidelines, and constraints for the review. Participants must be carefully selected to ensure that the best insights and judgments are brought to bear fairly on the issues. A competent study leader and good staff support are essential to success.

Third, any assessment is stressful for those under review. To ensure accurate information and interpretation and to avoid undue tension, the university's experience strongly supports the wisdom of allowing those affected by assessment to have the opportunity to present information and examine other information introduced for accuracy. Interpretation is, of course, the responsibility of the assessment team, but opportunities for comment before taking action can instill confidence in the assessment process.

Fourth, where faculty or staff experience with assessment is limited, it is prudent to concentrate initially on only one type of assessment to gain confidence and to overcome some of the inevitable concern for what may appear to be a threatening activity. Other assessments can then follow. On campuses with long experience in peer review of academic personnel and academic program review, the extension of assessment activities to administrative services, resource use, and policy review is less difficult.

Fifth, where assessment is well executed and subsequent responses in planning and resource management reflect its conclusions, criticism of institutional management from both internal and external sources seems to be reduced. What remains can usually be resolved in an atmosphere of objective self-analysis and constructive criticism.

10

Management and Leadership Strategies in Action

Some readers of the previous chapters may agree that the "Stage Three" approach to management during an era of uncertainty is desirable but fear that its introduction is impractical in the midst of serious financial constraints and the scramble to react to worsening economic and enrollment pressures. Admittedly, concern about institutional survival is overwhelming. As one university president has expressed it, "I know I should be looking ahead to the 1990s, but the present has to come first."

Our response to this concern is that management practices advocated in the preceding chapters are the most practical of any for such an era, albeit with intense commitment and effort. The essence of these management practices is management by anticipation. Odiorne (1981, p. 174) contrasts this approach to that of crisis management, in which "planning, thinking, reflection, invention, and creativity . . . are likely to disappear." Colleges and universities whose leaders fall into crisis management rather than actively planning for change are experiencing increasing difficulties in coping with present challenges and weakening their ability to survive.

A time of uncertainty allows leaders to make creative changes if they take advantage of opportunities that arise despite financial constraint. Dynamic planning as described in Chapters Three and Four can help administrators and faculty leaders develop more options, gain a greater sense of control over events, and be less reactive to those that cannot be controlled. The task of reviewing, refining, and reshaping goals and objectives as circumstances change—a more frequent and narrowly constrained task than in the growth era—keeps the range of vision of institutional leaders broad and moving. Not incidentally, the task provides extensive opportunities for leaders to communicate their aspirations and outlook. It also can foster greater institutional cohesion and *esprit de corps,* build a closer sense of identity, avoid focusing on what cannot be done rather than on what can, present positive rather than negative challenges to faculty and staff, and guide the allocation of resources in more effective and efficient directions. Reducing the effects of shocks and surprises is essential in managing, particularly under uncertainty. By keeping change more or less constant and incremental, even when drastic action must be taken, planning can remove much of the trauma endemic in crisis management.

The multiyear resource management processes outlined in Chapters Six and Seven can give leaders the needed resource flexibility to use unforeseen opportunities in moving toward desired goals, decrease risks by increasing resource availability to meet unforeseen problems, and lead to more effective resource use. Similarly, the assessment of results as illustrated in Chapters Eight and Nine can guide change and provide early indication of problems for which anticipatory planning provides a range of possible responses. The five types of review mechanisms advocated in those chapters can narrow the inconsistencies and anomalies that often inhibit full use of available resources.

When such feedback information is distributed to those close to the point of action, their corrective responses can be quick, small, and constant (Odiorne, 1981).

Careful planning, strategic use of resources, and evaluation of results can enable even those institutions now in difficulty to assure their long-term viability by setting internal expenditure priorities, cutting back on the size and scope of low-priority programs, sharing financial resources among departments, and raising additional funds from new sources. They can develop their comparative advantage by assessing their strengths and weaknesses within the context of their unique objectives. They can build on strengths by eliminating programs not central to their mission and by using economic incentives to encourage a desirable configuration of programs and resources.

Leadership for Change

The benefits of improved approaches to management are obvious. But what is needed to implement them? Clearly leadership plays the primary role. It is the chief executive who ensures that objectives and strategies are set. He must establish processes to see that resources are used to achieve objectives efficiently and effectively. He is responsible for seeing that performance is assessed routinely, and he selects persons for critical positions and provides the opportunity for their growth in those positions. He is the ultimate—and sensitive—arbiter of conflicts arising from incompatible or opposing needs of constituents. These are the primary leadership tasks required for instituting and accomplishing change.

Opportunities for Leadership. Within some constraints, management structure and style reflect the personality and preferences of the chief executive. He or she sets the tone and direction for the campus not only by what is delegated to whom but by communication mechanisms established, consultation orchestrated, decision processes used, and policy guidance provided. His or her influence is modified by sharing governance with faculty and, whatever the extent, shared governance introduces potential tensions at the boundaries of participation. These tensions and compromises should not be interpreted as lack of leadership, particularly during times of severe financial stringency. In the final analysis, the chief executive retains the power of the purse. Although the contents of the purse may be diminished, its power is still sufficient to provide the checks and balances necessary for determining institutional direction. Management of financial resources to achieve academic change is a powerful and underdeveloped tool available to chief executives and other academic managers. Administrative officers can significantly influence what disciplines should be emphasized; what types of student (such as undergraduate, graduate, or professional) are given priority; the size, number, and array of given programs; and the quality of all programs. They can influence programs through establishing new procedures for program approval, questioning program plans and operations, focusing academic program reviews on quality, and increasing interchange with academic deans to communicate program problems and objectives, as well as by direct intervention in resource allocations. Teaching, research, and consulting responsibilities of faculty can be influenced by criteria imposed in judging faculty performance, in setting compensation and benefit levels, and in allocating faculty time.

For example, a new president recently let it be known that he proposed to recruit more research-oriented faculty members and to shift the image of the institution from its traditional emphasis on teaching toward multiple objectives. This announcement itself was interpreted by faculty members as a major revision in promotion criteria. They responded by placing less emphasis on their commitment to undergraduate students and have begun to plan research activities and expanded graduate programs. The president's goal will undoubtedly be reinforced within two or three years as individual personnel actions give greater weight to scholarly publication and creativity than in prior years. In contrast, another president has embarked on a program of placing greater emphasis on documenting instructional performance and reviewing the relative time faculty members spend in the classroom. Not only do such policies change the behavior of existing faculty members, but they convey a sense of "what counts" to new faculty and to the public at large.

Next to salary and time, space is probably the most sensitive resource for an academician, particularly a "bench scientist." One economist has suggested that space, rather than money, could easily be the "medium of exchange" in universities. Thus, even space can be a valuable management tool to accomplish specific academic objectives, entice and retain particularly able scholars, and strengthen institutional quality. Rather than being powerless in affecting institutional directions, administrators retain an extensive array of incentives with which to influence change.

Talents of Leadership. Successful leadership blends rational management processes with political skill and acumen to effect change. That is, the processes and structures for planning, managing resources, and assessing results can be designed logically so that (1) they are clearly understood and accepted as legitimate; (2) problems arising within the institution are handled expeditiously in the appropriate sequence by the right people; and (3) similar problems arising at different points in time are handled consistently. When these management procedures and arrangements are clear and consistent, the probability is high that objectives and strategies emerging from planning will be accepted and applied, resource decisions will lead to goal achievement, and assessment processes will provide factual information for future actions with a minimum of resistance and subterfuge. But the decisions reached and the actions taken on the basis of these processes are most likely to be effective in achieving their goals if leaders use personal interaction, tact, persuasion, power, interpersonal sensitivity, negotiation, and compromise—definitely political skills.

Effective college and university presidents understand that decisions among competing interests must be reached and implemented by political processes—*political* meaning the total complex of relations among people rather than conflict resolution through expedient, short-run, and self-serving measures. When decisions are the result of both rational procedures and persuasive arguments, even difficult choices between competing programs and people are hard to fault or undo. By themselves, either rational procedures or political approaches are inadequate. On the one hand, substituting political machination and manipulation for logic and careful analysis can compromise the integrity of administrators and destroy their base of support. On the other, when leaders rely totally on the strength of rational procedures and overlook the political opportunities, they and their institution may suffer in the competition for resources and support. A lengthy history of rational arguments supported by careful analysis makes the use of political power far more effective.

The vast majority of administrators know the importance of legitimate decision-making procedures and political persuasion, but many of them doubt their ability to apply these techniques successfully in the face of looming stringencies. As one university president put it, "I have the hardware to manage effectively. It's the software I lack." The managerial talents that he and other administrative leaders need to make and implement difficult reallocation choices through the management cycle are numerous, but they can be learned. They are neither arcane nor innate. Among them, two are absolutely essential in applying an integrated approach to planning, resource management, and assessment. One of them, toward the rational and analytic side, is the talent of gaining good information. The other, toward the political side, is the ability to involve trustees, faculty, and other constituent groups productively in the management cycle.

Information

Effective management obviously requires accurate and timely information. But top administrators and policy groups need different information from that commonly available to them (Arrow, 1963).

First of all, their information needs differ from those of operating units. One of the most serious deficiencies in management information systems has been their reliance on data-gathering and analysis systems designed for day-to-day operations. As a result, more raw data than information have been available to key administrators and policy makers. For example, department and program heads use very detailed financial data and frequently unquantified information about individual faculty members and students to help make programmatic decisions on course offerings and faculty hiring. College deans need information on departmental enrollments, program quality, and trends in faculty workload for resource allocation and planning. But presidents or chancellors require quite different information to develop planning guidelines and policy parameters for the campus, allocate resources to meet campus goals, and assess resource use and policies ranging from space utilization to research contracts and grants in order to determine whether institutional objectives are being met at an acceptable rate. Conventional payroll and personnel data systems illustrate how operating-level data fail to meet the needs of top administrators. These systems contain a plethora of information about the characteristics of each employee—sex, age, ethnic identity, Social Security number, title code, status, fund and account source, and more. All this information is needed for functional managers to do their jobs. But top administrators need little information on particular individuals for their tasks. Instead, they need group data on trends such as faculty age distribution, projected turnover, and related costs. Existing systems can provide great detail on individuals, but the software to transform these data about individuals into information for use by policy makers is often lacking. A separate, though not complicated, system is required to produce an age distribution and projected turnover analysis of faculty. This is the type of personnel information that chief administrators most often need.

The time requirements of top administrators for such information are also very different from those of administrators of operating units. For policy analysis, there is often not time for a cautious accounting of how every last cent has been spent. Academic administrators ask a different type of question than accountants. For example, they need broad indications of where funds are going in support of major activities, even if a high degree of accuracy in these data must be forgone. Equally important, they need environmental information such as indicators of the labor market, federal funding, and political and economic trend indicators not found in institutional data produced by operational data systems. If data provided by operational systems are viewed as the exclusive sources for management information, then only a part of the information managers need will be available to them.

Part of the problem with getting useful information is that top administrators seldom decide precisely what information they need. As part of their faith in the science of data processing, they have assumed that critical performance variables will somehow be defined in the process of obtaining and analyzing computerized data. Thus, "needs assessments" have too often been left in the hands of systems analysts whose penchant has been to collect everything because someone someday may ask the right question. And decisions about how to define "full-time students" and to compare "credit hours" to "class hours" have been considered less academic policy decisions than mere decisions of data definition. This absence of policy decisions by managers about how to define, assemble, and present data in order to exercise leadership has had a serious side effect. Technical staff have tended to make independent decisions on what is appropriate. Yet these staff are seldom competent to make what amount to policy decisions. They lack sufficient experience with academic program management to grasp the usefulness and limitations of the data and they tend to be overconfident with the meaning, validity, and interpretation of quantitative data. Hoos (1977, p. 9) has commented that "preoccupation with numbers has subverted educational theory and philosophy. Accountability substitutes for integrity; the final accounting is a printout that, like an infinite hall of mirrors of self-reflection, creates only an endless regress. The cause of efficiency may thus be served, but the costs are incalculable and will have to be borne by the whole society, now and in the future." A false sense of security has come from implicitly assuming that computers produce information that is better than that obtained elsewhere. The numbers that appear on cathode-ray tubes and computer printouts appear to be "objective" data, containing important facts and constituting revealed truth on which hard choices can be soundly based. This is simply not true.

Most administrators have gained the wisdom—sometimes

by sad experience—to recognize the limitations as well as the power of computers. Computers can organize data quickly and (one hopes) inexpensively return them in any specified format, once the rules for organizing them are determined. Managers—not technical staff nor systems analysts—have to provide rules and define formats to generate useful information for monitoring and controlling. Only then can operating systems, reporting systems, and analytical systems be developed to support management activities.

Many managers have also learned that building comprehensive, fully integrated computerized information systems is not always the best solution to information needs. Preparing occasional reports by hand, sampling only a portion of cases, and using one-time surveys to handle issues not likely to recur are all methods of information gathering that are simpler and cheaper than comprehensive systems and equally adequate for some purposes. As Arrow notes, "A relatively small amount of information, properly chosen, may have large incentive effects" (1963, p. 20). A random audit of three or four departments for policy compliance can stimulate greater compliance by all.

In sum, adopting a more systematic approach to the planning, resource management, and assessment cycle does require new and more targeted information specified by decision makers, information that will come from a number of sources. Information needs will not be met solely by adopting large-scale computerized data systems. Equally important, in contrast to some administrators' fears, the more systematic approach does not require quantification of institutional or educational outcomes.

Howard Bowen (1977) and other economists agree that higher education must be accountable to its constituents and its benefactors but that to meet its responsibilities to develop human intellect, personality, and values, its operations cannot be determined by quantifiable data about its impact. The joint products and multiple objectives characterizing higher education are not easily quantifiable in theory, let alone in practice. Thus, as Bowen points out, administrators should not expect to develop, in an accounting sense, direct and reliable comparison of costs and outcomes. Prudent administrators "arrive at decisions by acquiring as much information or evidence as possible and then rely on informed judgment—a combination of sensitivity, insight, logical inference, and common sense" (1977, p. 22). To accept the notion that lack of measurability renders such information invalid would deny higher education leaders use of some of their most essential information. Emphasis on measurement—a by-product of the intense development of natural sciences and technology in the past forty years—has contributed greatly to human knowledge and well-being. But it has dominated thought in many other fields to the point at which they are in danger of losing valuable perspective on the issues they must deal with. More opportunity exists to improve management in higher education by integrating quantitative and qualitative information in assessment processes than by concentrating efforts on gathering only quantifiable data about higher education outcomes.

No magic ways exist to get information with which to answer the hard questions of how to encourage institutional vitality and assess institutional effectiveness. Some administrators tend to retreat from decisions about these issues because they do not think they know enough about them. What they must understand is that information is only a companion to experienced and enlightened judgment. It is not, nor should it inadvertently become, a surrogate for judgment.

The Politics of Change

Administrative officers may occasionally retire to the quiet of their studies and emerge with decisions that are theirs alone. But while they have lonely responsibility for many decisions, they are rarely alone in reaching them. Most major institutional decisions involve and benefit from the participation of trustees, faculty, staff, and students, and effective administrators try to organize this participation so that it is both most useful and economical.

This diffuse and intricate process for reaching decisions makes academic management distinctly different from management in either business or government organizations. Many corporations and government agencies are as complex as universities in terms of purpose, structure, personnel, and operating processes. A large number of them must also plan and manage multiple fund sources as well as meet multiple objectives. More and more of them have decentralized their decision making. But just as the intangible nature of end products in education contrasts sharply with the tangible output of most industrial, commercial, and service enterprises and government offices, the shared responsibility in management decisions between administrators and faculty of colleges and universities is vastly different from that existing between management and labor in the private sector or between officials and staff in government. Further, once decisions have been made, there are innumerable opportunities for the intent of the decisions to be subverted as external agencies and internal political coalitions work to modify them.

Business and industrial leaders and public officials often criticize the extensive, time-consuming consultation and seeming lack of clear authority characteristic of academic governance as indications of poor management. Academics themselves sometimes describe their management environment in exasperation as one of "organized anarchy" (Cohen and March, 1974). Jacques Barzun (1968, p. 96) captures the essence of academic management as "a congeries of persons and devices. What is known on campuses as 'central administration' is but one part; and its ostensible power, derived from the trustees and based on a few statutes, is little more than a concentration of *influence.* ... When one looks for the administration at a given university, one must knock at almost every other door." This amorphous leadership structure, characteristic of only a few organizations, such as universities, hospitals, and research institutes whose function is to coordinate the work of a group of associated professionals, means that the role of the college or university executive can be fully appreciated only in the context of what the governing board, faculty, staff, and students are expected to contribute to administrative decisions. It also means that success in this role depends on involving the right people at the right time and in the right way in the planning, resource management, and assessment cycle.

Most academic administrators have been successful faculty members, but ironically, some of the qualities that made them such—a strong sense of working independently, self-reliance, and confidence in their own ability to manage details—frequently interfere with their ability to involve others easily in decisions and to delegate authority effectively. They may unwittingly adopt a centralized style of crisis management on the grounds that institutional problems are so complex and events so uncertain and fast-changing that consultative approaches are not going to be effective. Some may adopt a "political" view of academic government (Baldridge and others, 1978) in which short-term political expediency dominates the legitimate political processes of negotiation, persuasion, and compromise. Moreover, they may see information as power and as a manipulative tool to be closely guarded and controlled as a means of attaining such power. They may keep assignments of responsibility unclear to diffuse responsibility while retaining centralized authority. They may appoint study groups or task forces as façades to "contain" sensitive problems while taking unilateral action on them. They may even create confusion and precipitate crises in order to use the turmoil to accomplish their own objectives.

A serious weakness of this politically expedient style of decision making is the suspicion it creates about whether leaders are acting in the best interests of the institution or merely in the interest of their own survival. Irrespective of individual motivation, the suspicion will persist as long as decisions and actions appear to be dominated by administrative fiat. A more serious result lies in the resistance to decisions that develops among those excluded from the process. Not only are the legitimacy and integrity of the process suspect in the eyes of nonparticipants, the validity of the decisions is rejected. Resistance to change in colleges and universities is deep-seated and common enough as is; it does not need the added burden of accusations of illegitimate decisions about change.

College and university leadership calls for the best political skills of administrators—not just expediency. Political acumen involves sensitivity to the politics of change. In 1513, Machiavelli wrote, "It must be considered that there is nothing more difficult to carry out, nor more doubtful of success, nor more dangerous to handle, than to initiate a new order of things. For the reformer has enemies in all those who profit by the old order, and only lukewarm defenders in all those who would profit by the new order, this lukewarmness arising partly from fear of their adversaries, who have the laws in their favor; and partly from the incredulity of mankind, who do not truly believe in anything new until they have had actual experience of it. Thus it arises that on every opportunity for attacking the reformer, his opponents do so with the zeal of partisans, the others only defend him half-heartedly, so that between them he runs great danger" ([1513], 1950, p. 21). A university president, more pressed for time, recently put the problem more succinctly: "Friends come and go; enemies accumulate."

Resistance to change of any kind is universal in all organizations, but because of the diffuse nature of academic government, faculty, staff, and other participants all have particular opportunity and right to resist change. Administrators must take this resistance into account in seeking to achieve change. Among the more important sources of resistance that they should consider are these:

- Instructional programs are managed directly by departmental faculty members who are likely to continue to do what they are doing unless incentives or persuasion convinces them otherwise. Administrative control over program funding is not absolute, particularly in the short run; hence the leverage of economic incentives is not complete.
- Students currently enrolled also have a stake in the continuation of programs essentially in the form that originally attracted them. Everyone recognizes that a substantial change in one program may have unexpected consequences for others and for students as well as faculty, through changes in demand for related courses, schedules, space requirements, and budgetary needs.
- Many staff members believe that little either can or should be changed. This is especially so among those in nonacademic middle-management positions. The bureaucratic envi-

ronment of these tasks produces this "anti-planner" orientation (Odiorne, 1981) because staff members get so enmeshed in detailed activity that they forget the organization's goals. The activity goes on; everyone is busy; but tangible outcomes and forward movement are often hard to detect.

Like everyone else, faculty, students, and staff approve of those changes they themselves create. However, when change is forced on them, resistance is strong. Innovators who forget this fact may not only fail to get their changes accepted but pay a personal or professional price for their attempt. Those who actively oppose the change may claim that it has already been tried before and failed, that it is "against policy," that others would never approve it, or that the motives of the proponent are suspect. Less active opponents may subvert the change either by encouraging endless debate over minor points or by simple defiance.

Resistance can be overcome, but to do so, innovators must lead resisters to see that the advantages of change are greater than its disadvantages. Skillful innovators know the futility of attempting to achieve major change in the absence of overwhelming evidence of a need to do so. Most important to this task is involving faculty and other groups in the planning, decision, and assessment process.

Increasing Faculty Involvement. Faculty members are the primary resource of educational institutions. They pride themselves on intellectual and professional independence and do not easily perceive themselves as subject to management. Successful administrators recognize this faculty perspective on its role and encourage, rather than discourage, a strong sense of professorial independence. At the same time, administrators understand that overall institutional performance depends on how well faculty talents and time are allocated and used. Sustaining high faculty morale by providing full information in essential matters, involving faculty appropriately in institutional decisions, and guarding faculty time by providing needed administrative support are key to successful academic administration. If faculty members are dissatisfied with institutional management, those who are mobile (often the most able) can accept employment elsewhere, while others subscribe to collective bargaining as the most immediate alternative.

The role of individual faculty members in university management is complex. Each is a professional with nearly absolute control over the conduct of instruction in the classroom and research in the laboratory or library. As members of academic departments, they share a common concern for the content of an academic program, recruitment of new faculty, student achievement, teaching assignments and schedules, and even division of assigned space, time, and support services. As members of faculty bodies such as academic senates, they may carry a broader campuswide responsibility for educational policy, admission and graduation requirements, personnel and program evaluation, and development of library, computer, and other academic support services. Appointment to faculty and administrative committees further draws faculty into management. Joining together independent of the institution for such purposes as legislative lobbying and collective bargaining involves them in additional decision processes, though potentially in an adversarial, rather than a participatory, role in the institution. The wide array of issues demanding informed academic judgment underscores both the complexities and the importance of faculty involvement in management.

Perhaps more than nonacademic staff, when institutional change is needed, faculty members respond to facts, logic, and persuasive argument. Hence, information analysis, discussion and debate are particularly essential for successful change involving the faculty. To create an awareness and understanding of issues among the faculty, forthright written statements by the president, face-to-face dialogue between administrators and faculty, well-prepared staff papers, and joint faculty-administrator task forces can all be used successfully.

All colleges and universities trying seriously to plan involve faculty members early in the planning process. Administrators have learned by experience to include them for the special talents they can bring to the resolution of issues as well as for their support. But administrators must not try to give the appearance of faculty involvement and consultation in decisions in which the faculty have really had no or limited participation, nor expect faculty members to defend and endorse such decisions. They may win faculty acquiescence in an occasional crisis decision when administrative response is required in a short time without the usual faculty consultation, but only if the faculty have earlier had the opportunity to consider plans and policy from which the decision flows.

Just as faculty members must participate in goal setting if they are to direct their efforts toward implementing them, once goals are set, their implementation and assessment of those goals must be legitimized. Faculty forums, faculty-administrator retreats, and cooperative refinement of draft policies are useful means of doing so. These processes are particularly important in preparing for possible retrenchment. The pitfalls of retrenchment are sufficiently numerous that administrators will be criticized for whatever actions they take. Consultation on priorities can be particularly useful in muting criticism if it occurs before cutbacks are imminent. Such early involvement is less important for winning faculty acceptance for reductions of budgets, positions, or programs—since after initial dissatisfaction, the faculty almost always accept the decisions—than it is for retaining high morale. Acceptance is not enough: Damage to faculty enthusiasm, initiative, and productivity can stem from less than satisfactory management of decline. Administrators who have successfully accomplished faculty termination because of financial exigency have found that the burden of proof is on them to demonstrate—almost to guarantee—that the net result will leave the institution as a whole better off than before. To do so, the logic for termination must be nearly overwhelming.

Institutions that have squarely faced the issue of retrenchment have typically been confronted with serious financial distress before their administrators and faculty joined together in planning and executing necessary changes. Other institutions would be well advised to organize careful faculty-administrator study of the future environment, institutional objectives, management practices and programmatic strengths and weaknesses before the onset of serious financial stress. Administrators have claimed that faculty members are unwilling to participate in analyses that may lead to retrenchment. But increasingly, individual faculty members and faculty senates are aware of the need for contingency planning. They are growing openly critical of administrative officers who lack resolve in facing the possibility of retrenchment. Faculty recognize that new and more dynamic approaches are required to induce change and that low-priority programs may have to be curtailed or eliminated to strengthen essential programs and develop new areas of knowledge that will contribute to the betterment of society. They understand that in many instances these ends can be accomplished only if internal reallocation of money and positions takes place, and they recognize that some tenured faculty members may have to be terminated. They see the merits of joint faculty and administrative planning of retrenchment, knowing that if evidence of better management is not forthcoming, loss of public confidence will lead to further financial erosion. Therefore, faculty leaders are beginning to call for somebody to "bite the bullet" before academic quality further erodes. They are looking to academic administrators for the needed leadership and yet are acutely concerned with establishing their role in managing retrenchment.

In sum, the uncertainties of the 1980s require extensive faculty involvement in academic planning, resource decisions, and assessment. Because unionization limits drastically the dimensions of shared governance, collective bargaining will largely negate the opportunities for extensive faculty participation in management activities. In contrast, if administrators inform the faculty members and assure their real participation cooperative methods to guide and achieve needed change should develop, and faculty support for change will follow.

Increasing Staff Participation. Enrollment growth rates in most colleges and universities since the 1950s have been paralleled, if not surpassed, by growth of administrative and academic support service staff and "functional managers"—assistant vice-presidents, assistants to various officers, directors, assistant directors, and coordinators, to name a few. This cadre of middle-level administrators and staff has evolved on many campuses into a necessary bureaucracy to manage a wide array of business services. Nearly all these managers and staff are career professionals in university administration.

Whether or not one agrees that the growth in this professional staff has been fully justified, its development has influenced college and university management significantly. Analytical strengths have increased within the administrative organization; student services have improved; external relations have been strengthened—all positive outcomes. Yet the balance of power between the faculty and administration has shifted in the direction of staff control; faculty suspicion has grown about administrative understanding of academic values and processes; and bureaucratic rigidities and compartmentalization have led to pursuit of narrow goals based partly on unit self-interest. Often, because of less than adequate management guidance, these units and their staff have only a narrow perspective about how their activities relate to institutional objectives. In the past, persons have been appointed to staff positions because of their specific technical skills but without adequate concern for their understanding of the academic environment. Without this understanding, their ability to adapt assigned tasks to new needs has been seriously compromised. Many overly circumscribe their activities because of limited knowledge of the full range of actions that they could take to achieve objectives.

Leaders must increase the understanding of these staff about the academic environment, recognize potential for growth among them, provide opportunities for growth, reward them on the basis of performance, and be prepared to dismiss them for inadequate performance. Developing their skills improves the quality of their work, increases faculty productivity, and reduces management costs.

Overcoming resistance to change among staff demands different strategies than among faculty. Staff are more often wedded to specific procedures than are faculty. To some staff, any attempt to introduce a new approach appears an attack on them for following an old approach. Getting the facts together to persuade staff of the need for change is not enough. The facts must be interpreted by top management and specific implications drawn with respect to present staff activities. Unlike faculty, staff expect clear direction by top management. They are accustomed to hierarchical organizational structures and to the delegation of responsibility and authority within the hierarchy. Thus, they will respond more positively than faculty to work assignments specified by administrators. Of course, like faculty, staff respond most favorably if they are given positive feedback for changing. Highlighting the favorable consequences of change and reducing its perceived risks can increase their cooperation.

Involving Other Groups. The faculty and staff are those who are involved with change on a day-to-day basis and whose individual careers are most directly affected. Therefore, administrators must plan their involvement in decisions. But governing boards, with their responsibility for oversight and policy direction, are equally important, since they must concur in and support the chief executive if any major change is to be achieved. Students may have legitimate concerns for changing programs and may suggest, support, or oppose changes. The chief executive must establish positive means for obtaining student perspective. The interests of external groups such as legislative committees, coordinating bodies, alumni, and various public interest groups are important and must be taken into account as the chief executive, together with his or her internal advisers, plans for change.

Governing boards, particularly of public institutions, have undergone important changes. Board members are increasingly drawn from a wider pool than the business and philanthropic groups that furnished the majority of board members in the past. Terms have been shortened in many institutions, requiring presidents and experienced trustees to spend more time in bringing new board members up to a basic threshold of knowledge about their institutions. Board meetings are subject to greater public attention as "sunshine laws" require open meetings. These changes have influenced the quality of debate, both positively and negatively.

Many presidents find it more difficult than it once was to share problems openly with their boards. Discussions are increasingly formal, for the participants often lack the benefit of common experience. Administrators can no longer turn automatically to board members for expert advice on questions of finance and management. Time and political acumen are needed to develop a solid working relationship in which the president can apprise the board of necessary policy changes and expect both constructive reaction and assistance.

Relationships with external groups—state/federal 1202 commissions, government at various levels, other colleges and universities, secondary schools, alumni, and the general public—are varied, complex, ever changing, and difficult to control. On controversial issues the chief executive is inevitably required to deal with several groups of concerned constituents, each advocating a different position. For example, possible changes in admission requirements may be seen by other colleges as a threat to their own future enrollments. Funding sources may take one position with respect to potential costs and another on the social desirability of the change. Secondary schools will interpret the change and react on the basis of its expected effect on their programs and students. Those in or out of the eligibility pool who expect to be affected will make their positions known, and the faculty will view any change as a raising or lowering of standards and will react accordingly. Each constituency will expect an "impartial" hearing and then action that matches its perception of what is "right."

Since gaining a stronger voice in the late 1960s and early 1970s, students have been added to some governing boards and are increasingly consulted on courses and the quality of instruction.

This environment requires careful planning and timely consultation. Each group requires individual attention in how it is approached and what is emphasized, but the information transmitted must be accurate and consistent both during the deliberations and once the decision to change is made.

Conclusion

Academic administrators often despair of managing a college or university to their own satisfaction, knowing the impossibility of managing the institution satisfactorily from everyone else's point of view. The approach to academic management presented here can provide administrators greater self-satisfaction while increasing acceptance of academic management by others. It emphasizes creativity rather than constraint, continuity rather than crisis, initiative rather than conformity, achievement rather than protocol.

The rate at which such an approach to planning, resource management, and assessment can be introduced in an institution depends on how well and how fast faculty and staff can accept broader and changing responsibilities, perform within policy guidance rather than procedural directives, respond to incentives rather than restrictions, and view circumstances and events as they are, not as they were in the past or as faculty and staff wish they were. Presidents must seek and appoint persons to whom they can delegate authority to help institute its processes at all levels and educate present faculty and staff in this direction.

Deans, department chairs, and other administrators who are attuned to institutional objectives and goals, who understand the need for and the methods of achieving change in academic institutions, and who have the respect and support of the faculty to do so are critical in instituting such an approach. Decentralizing authority and rewarding leadership performance at all levels will help attract the most able academic managers.

To adopt this dynamic, cyclic approach to planning, resource management, and assessment of necessity requires education. But the job of the university is education. Faculty, staff, and administrators must be educated to keep their skills current, increase their responsibilities, and cooperate in achieving common goals; and a systematic approach to the management cycle can aid this education. Education is not by lecture but by policies and practices that reinforce planning, self-evaluation, and self-development. Just as this management approach supports continuous institutional renewal through a never-ending cycle of analysis, action, and adaptation to new challenges, so it can contribute to individual growth and renewal among all members of the institution—trustees, administrators, and students as well as faculty and staff—so that the process of change is continuous and dynamic.

The leadership styles of college and university leaders must change as well. The charismatic leader of the forties and fifties gave way to the hardened negotiator in the sixties and the compromiser in the seventies. Leaders in the eighties must be statesmen in the true sense of the word—regarded as unbiased promoters of the public good. These "statesman-leaders" will have to take more risks than their predecessors if they are truly dedicated to the continuing vitality of their institutions. They will have to rethink the way colleges and universities do business and stress the need not only for presidents to be statesmen but also for faculty, outside policy makers, and those who provide resources to be statesmen as well. We believe that only then will universities be able to consolidate past strengths and build new ones to meet changing objectives and future challenges.

Bibliographical
Resources on
Academic Management

This short essay cites some particularly important historical and contemporary sources helpful in understanding and improving management in higher education. It is organized similarly to the presentation of topics in this book and is included to help those who wish further information about these topics.

The Nature of Higher Education

To understand the need for improved management and the possibilities and limitations that constitute reality in colleges and universities, a number of works should be high-priority reading. They are listed here in order of relevance to this book. Full publication information can be found in the list of references that follows this essay.

Jacques Barzun, *The American University* (1968).
Clark Kerr, *The Uses of the University* (1963).
David D. Henry, *Challenges Past, Challenges Present: An Analysis of American Higher Education Since 1930* (1975).
John D. Millett, *New Structures of Campus Power: Success and Failures of Emerging Forms of Institutional Governance* (1978).
Eugene C. Lee and Frank M. Bowen, *Managing Multicampus Systems: Effective Administration in an Unsteady State* (1975).
Carnegie Council on Policy Studies in Higher Education, *Three Thousand Futures: The Next Twenty Years for Higher Education* (1980).

The many volumes of the Carnegie Commission on Higher Education and the Carnegie Council on Policy Studies in Higher Education present the most comprehensive and analytical treatment of the many changes in the managerial environment of higher education and the more intransigent public policy issues it faces. Many of these volumes offer important recommended changes in both governmental and institutional policies.

General Management

Classic references on general management that we believe are most insightful include:

Harold Koontz and Cyril O'Donnell, *Principles of Management* (1976).
Amitai Etzioni, *Modern Organizations* (1964).
C. West Churchman, *The Systems Approach* (1968).
George S. Odiorne, *Management by Objectives* (1965).
Anthony Downs, *Inside Bureaucracy* (1967).
Peter F. Drucker, *Management: Tasks, Responsibilities, Practices* (1974).
Joseph W. McGuire (Ed.), *Contemporary Management: Issues and Viewpoints* (1974).

Several new titles update these classic ideas about management and decision making. Those most relevant to the theme of this book include:

C. H. Levine, "Organizational Decline and Cutback Management," *Public Administration Review* (1978).
Peter F. Drucker, *Managing in Turbulent Times* (1980).
George S. Odiorne, *The Change Resisters* (1981).

Higher Education Management

The past decade has produced a number of books examining management in higher education, resulting in an extended understanding of its complexities, power politics and conflict, and opportunities for improvement. Some particularly helpful volumes are:

Kenneth P. Mortimer and T. R. McConnell, *Sharing Authority Effectively: Participation, Interaction, and Discretion* (1978).
John D. Millett, *New Structures of Campus Power: Success and Failures of Emerging Forms of Institutional Governance* (1978).
J. Victor Baldridge, *Power and Conflict in the University: Research in the Sociology of Complex Organizations* (1971).
Frederick E. Balderston, *Managing Today's University* (1974).
Barry M. Richman and Richard N. Farmer, *Leadership, Goals, and Power in Higher Education: A Contingency and Open-Systems Approach to Effective Management* (1974).
Paul Jedamus, Marvin W. Peterson, and Associates, *Improving Academic Management: A Handbook of Planning and Institutional Research* (1980).

Dynamic Planning

The planning literature has expanded rapidly as a result of new challenges to management in all types of organizations and of increased difficulty in defining and setting goals as organizations have become more complex and bureaucratic and in recognition of the new planning tools—many with stochastic properties—now available. Six references are particularly helpful in understanding planning in complex organizations:

D. E. Hussey, *Introducing Corporate Planning* (1979).
James B. Quinn, *Strategies for Change: Logical Incrementalism* (1980).
George A. Steiner, *Top Management Planning* (1969).
Norman P. Uhl, *Encouraging Convergence of Opinion Through the Use of the Delphi Technique in the Process of Identifying an Institution's Goals* (1971).
Eugene C. Lee and Frank M. Bowen, *Managing Multicampus Systems: Effective Administration in an Unsteady State* (1975).
Stephen A. Hoenack, "Direct and Incentive Planning Within a University," *Socio-Economic Planning Science* (1977).

The newer planning tools reflect a desire to join strategic planning to clearer goal identification and resource estimation as a logical and integrated set of activities. Mathematical planning models specific to college and university management have been designed during the past decade. But their impact on decision making has been important only in isolated instances. The best of these models, in our opinion, are presented in the following:

William F. Massy, "A Dynamic Equilibrium Model for University Budget Planning," *Management Science* (1976).
David S. P. Hopkins, J. Larreche, and William F. Massy, "Constrained Optimization of a University Administration's Preference Function," *Management Science* (1977).

These models and others designed to guide management decisions in higher education institutions have contributed to a clearer understanding of the nature of decisions that must be made, complex factors that must be taken into account, and extensive ramifications that given decisions may have now and in the future. In time, mathematical models may be developed sufficiently to guide academic managers directly in resource management decisions. Three kinds of shortcomings must be resolved first: (1) aggregation of data necessary to apply mathematical models immediately forces together noncomparable information and masks many of the essential resource differences between programs, (2) an assumption of these models is that resource decisions can be optimal if they are centrally determined, which is counter to the way universities are structured and managed, and (3) the nonquantifiable inputs and outcomes limit the potential for comprehensiveness of these models and their ability to approximate reality.

Resource Management

Paralleling the activity of those interested in mathematical models have been a number of significant additions to the literature of resource management and control in higher education. Six we believe to be particularly interesting and illustrative:

Meredith A. Gonyea, "Determining Academic Staff Needs, Allocation, and Utilization," in P. Jedamus, M. W. Peterson, and Associates, *Improving Academic Management: A Handbook of Planning and Institutional Research* (1980).
Charles S. Benson, Jo M. Ritzen, and Irene Blumenthal, "Recent Perspectives in the Economics of Education," *Social Science Quarterly* (1974).
Roger G. Schroeder, "Resource Planning in University Management by Goal Programming," *Operations Research* (1974).
Frank M. Bowen and Sandra O. Archibald, "University Budgeting in an Era of Scarce Resources," in Craig Michalak (Ed.), *Managing Tomorrow's University* (1977).
Richard C. Grinold, David S. P. Hopkins, and William F. Massy, "A Model for Long-Range University Budget Planning Under Uncertainty," *Bell Journal of Economics* (1978).

Performance Assessment

The literature on assessing performance in higher education emphasizes single facets of the total college or university operations, with limited reference to the relationships between assessment and planning and resource use. Assessing specific activities such as personnel performance and program review has been examined, some of the more informative titles being:

Frank M. Bowen and Lyman A. Glenny, *Quality and Accountability: An Evaluation of Statewide Program Review Procedures* (1981).
Harold Koontz, *Appraising Managers as Managers* (1981).
Eugene C. Craven (Ed.), *New Directions for Institutional Research: Alternative Models of Academic Program Evaluation* (1980).
Harold L. Hodgkinson and others, *Improving and Assessing Performance: Evaluation in Higher Education* (1975).
John A. Centra, *Determining Faculty Effectiveness: Assessing Teaching, Research, and Service for Personnel Decisions and Improvement* (1979).
Howard R. Bowen, *Investment in Learning: The Individual and Social Value of American Higher Education* (1977).
C. Robert Pace, *Measuring Outcomes of College: Fifty Years of Findings and Recommendations for the Future* (1979).
Howard R. Bowen (Ed.), *New Directions for Institutional Research: Evaluating Institutions for Accountability* (1974).
Peter F. Drucker, *Managing for Results* (1964).
Paul L. Dressel, *Handbook of Academic Evaluation: Assessing Institutional Effectiveness, Student Progress, and Professional Performance for Decision Making in Higher Education* (1976).
University of Wisconsin, *Summary of University of Wisconsin System Academic Program Audit and Review* (1977).
University of California, *Handbook of Program Review* (1978).
Aaron Wildavsky, "The Self-Evaluating Organization," *Public Administration Review* (1972).

Not enough has been done in higher education in assessing resource use or reviewing policy systematically; yet these dimensions of assessment are essential to the management cycle. Though certainly not directly applicable, much can be learned from the private sector, where evaluation and feedback of results to inform planning and resource management are used extensively. Suggested further readings include:

Frederick E. Balderston, *Thinking About the Outputs of Higher Education* (1970).
Peter A. Phyrr, *Zero-Base Budgeting: A Practical Management Tool for Evaluating Expenses* (1973).
Meredith A. Gonyea (Ed.), *New Directions for Institutional Research: Analyzing and Constructing Cost* (1978).
Leonard Merewitz and Steven H. Sosnick, *The Budget's New Clothes* (1971).
Kenneth J. Arrow, "Control in Large Organizations" (1963).
Harold Koontz and Robert W. Bradspies, "Managing Through Feedforward Control: A Future-Directed View," *Business Horizons* (1972).
George B. Weathersby and Frederick E. Balderston, "PPBS in Higher Education Planning and Management," *Higher Education* (1972).

Leadership Strategy and Implementing Change

Planning, resource management, and assessment are useful insofar as they lead to accomplishment of desired change in an organization. Their effectiveness depends on leaders' qualities and skills in developing and implementing strategies to achieve changing objectives. The literature on organizational leadership reflects the complex relationships characteristic of shared governance, the importance of leadership style, and the critical role of information. Some suggested readings include:

J. Victor Baldridge, *Power and Conflict in the University: Research in the Sociology of Complex Organizations* (1971).
Charles E. Lindblom, *The Policy Making Process* (1968).

Harold L. Hodgkinson and L. Richard Meeth (Eds.), *Power and Authority: Transformation of Campus Governance* (1971).

Roger W. Heyns (Ed.), *Leadership of Higher Education* (1976).

Barry M. Richman and Richard N. Farmer, *Leadership, Goals, and Power in Higher Education: A Contingency and Open-Systems Approach to Effective Management* (1974).

Donald E. Walker, *The Effective Administrator: A Practical Approach to Problem Solving, Decision Making, and Campus Leadership* (1979).

George S. Odiorne, *The Change Resisters* (1981).

Alexander W. Astin and Rita A. Scherrei, *Maximizing Leadership Effectiveness: Impact of Administrative Style on Faculty and Students* (1980).

Sherman S. Blumenthal, *Management Information Systems: A Framework for Planning and Development* (1969).

G. Anthony Gorry and Michael S. Morton, "A Framework for Management Information Systems," *Sloan Management Review* (1971).

Robert G. Murdick, "MIS for MBO," *Journal of Systems Management* (1977).

J. J. Alexander, *Information Systems Analysis* (1974).

Carl R. Adams (Ed.), *New Directions for Institutional Research: Appraising Information Needs of Decision Makers* (1977).

❧❧❧ References

Adams, C. R. (Ed.). *New Directions for Institutional Research: Appraising Information Needs of Decision Makers,* no. 15. San Francisco: Jossey-Bass, 1977.

Alexander, J. J. *Information Systems Analysis.* Palo Alto, Calif.: Science Research Associates, 1974.

Arrow, K. J. *Control in Large Organizations.* Technical Report No. 123. Stanford, Calif.: Institute for Mathematical Studies in the Social Sciences, Stanford University, 1963.

Astin, A. W., and Scherrei, R. A. *Maximizing Leadership Effectiveness: Impact of Administrative Style on Faculty and Students.* San Francisco: Jossey-Bass, 1980.

Balderston, F. E. *Thinking About the Outputs of Higher Education.* Report No. P-5. Berkeley, Calif.: Ford Foundation Program for Research in University Administration, 1970.

Balderston, F. E. *Managing Today's University.* San Francisco: Jossey-Bass, 1974.

Baldridge, J. V. *Power and Conflict in the University: Research in the Sociology of Complex Organizations.* New York: Wiley, 1971.

Baldridge, J. V., and others. *Policy Making and Effective Lead-*

ership: A National Study of Academic Management. San Francisco: Jossey-Bass, 1978.

Barzun, J. *The American University.* New York: Harper & Row, 1968.

Benson, C. S., Ritzen, J. M., and Blumenthal, I. "Recent Perspectives in the Economics of Education." *Social Science Quarterly,* 1974, *52*(2), 244-261.

Blumenthal, S. S. *Management Information Systems: A Framework for Planning and Development.* Englewood Cliffs, N.J.: Prentice-Hall, 1969.

Bowen, F. M., and Archibald, S. O. "University Budgeting in an Era of Scarce Resources." In C. Michalak (Ed.), *Managing Tomorrow's University.* Riverside: University of California Academic Business Officers, 1977.

Bowen, F. M., and Glenny, L. A. *Quality and Accountability: An Evaluation of Statewide Program Review Procedures.* Sacramento: California Postsecondary Education Commission, 1981.

Bowen, H. R. (Ed.). *New Directions for Institutional Research: Evaluating Institutions for Accountability,* no. 1. San Francisco: Jossey-Bass, 1974.

Bowen, H. R. *Investment in Learning: The Individual and Social Value of American Higher Education.* San Francisco: Jossey-Bass, 1977.

Breneman, D. W., and Finn, C. E., Jr. *Public and Private Higher Education.* Washington, D.C.: Brookings Institution, 1978.

California State Department of Education. *Racial and Ethnic Survey, 1967-1973.* Sacramento: State of California, 1977.

Carnegie Council on Policy Studies in Higher Education. *Three Thousand Futures: The Next Twenty Years for Higher Education.* San Francisco: Jossey-Bass, 1980.

Cartter, A. "Graduate Education and Research in the Decades Ahead." In A. C. Eurick (Ed.), *Campus 1980.* New York: Delacorte Press, 1968.

Centra, J. A. *Determining Faculty Effectiveness: Assessing Teaching, Research, and Service for Personnel Decisions and Improvement.* San Francisco: Jossey-Bass, 1979.

Cheit, E. F. *The New Depression in Higher Education.* San Francisco: Jossey-Bass, 1971.

Churchman, C. W. *The Systems Approach.* New York: Dela-corte Press, 1968.

Cohen, M. D., and March, J. G. *Leadership and Ambiguity: The American College President.* New York: McGraw-Hill, 1974.

Craven, E. C. "A Concluding Perspective." In E. C. Craven (Ed.), *New Directions for Institutional Research: Alternative Models of Academic Program Evaluation,* no. 27. San Francisco: Jossey-Bass, 1980.

Cyert, R. M. Review of Balderston, F. E., *Managing Today's University. Journal of Economic Literature,* 1978, *16*(1), 159-160.

Cyert, R. M., Simon, H. A., and Trow, D. B. "Observation of a Business Division." *Journal of Business,* October 1956, pp. 237-248.

Downs, A. *Inside Bureaucracy.* Boston: Little, Brown, 1967.

Dressel, P. L. *Handbook of Academic Evaluation: Assessing Institutional Effectiveness, Student Progress, and Professional Performance for Decision Making in Higher Education.* San Francisco: Jossey-Bass, 1976.

Drucker, P. F. *Managing for Results.* New York: Harper & Row, 1964.

Drucker, P. F. *Management: Tasks, Responsibilities, Practices.* New York: Harper & Row, 1974.

Drucker, P. F. *Managing in Turbulent Times.* New York: Harper & Row, 1980.

Etzioni, A. *Modern Organizations.* Englewood Cliffs, N.J.: Prentice-Hall, 1964.

Gonyea, M. A. (Ed.). *New Directions for Institutional Research: Analyzing and Constructing Cost,* no. 17. San Francisco: Jossey-Bass, 1978.

Gonyea, M. A. "Determining Academic Staff Needs, Allocation, and Utilization." In P. Jedamus, M. W. Peterson, and Associates, *Improving Academic Management: A Handbook of Planning and Institutional Research.* San Francisco: Jossey-Bass, 1980.

Gorry, G. A., and Morton, M. S. "A Framework for Management Information Systems." *Sloan Management Review,* 1971, *13*(1), 55-70.

Greiner, L. E. "Evolution and Revolution as Organizations

Grow." In *Harvard Business Review on Management.* New York: Harper & Row, 1975.

Grinold, R. C., Hopkins, D. S. P., and Massy, W. F. "A Model for Long-Range University Budget Planning Under Uncertainty." *Bell Journal of Economics,* 1978, *9*(2), 396-420.

Henry, D. D. *Challenges Past, Challenges Present: An Analysis of American Higher Education Since 1930.* San Francisco: Jossey-Bass, 1975.

Heyns, R. W. (Ed.). *Leadership of Higher Education.* Washington, D.C.: American Council on Education, 1976.

Hodgetts, R. M. *Management Fundamentals.* Hinsdale, Ill.: Dryden Press, 1980.

Hodgkinson, H. L., and Meeth, L. R. (Eds.). *Power and Authority: Transformation of Campus Governance.* San Francisco: Jossey-Bass, 1971.

Hodgkinson, H. L., and others. *Improving and Assessing Performance: Evaluation in Higher Education.* Berkeley: Center for Research and Development in Higher Education, University of California, 1975.

Hoenack, S. A. "Direct and Incentive Planning Within a University." *Socio-Economic Planning Science,* 1977, *2,* 191-204.

Hoos, I. R. "The Costs of Efficiency—Implications of Educational Technology." Unpublished paper, Berkeley, Calif., 1977.

Hopkins, D. S. P., Larreche, J., and Massy, W. F. "Constrained Optimization of a University Administration's Preference Function." *Management Science,* 1977, *24*(4), 365-377.

Hopkins, D. S. P., and Schroeder, R. G. (Eds.). *New Directions for Institutional Research: Applying Analytic Methods to Planning and Management,* no. 13. San Francisco: Jossey-Bass, 1977.

Hussey, D. E. *Introducing Corporate Planning.* (2nd ed.) Oxford, England: Pergamon Press, 1979.

Jedamus, P., Peterson, M. W., and Associates. *Improving Academic Management: A Handbook of Planning and Institutional Research.* San Francisco: Jossey-Bass, 1980.

Kerr, C. *The Uses of the University.* Cambridge, Mass.: Harvard University Press, 1963.

Koontz, H. *Appraising Managers as Managers.* New York: McGraw-Hill, 1981.

Koontz, H., and Bradspies, R. W. "Managing Through Feedforward Control: A Future-Directed View." *Business Horizons,* 1972, *15*(3), 25-36.

Koontz, H., and O'Donnell, C. *Principles of Management.* New York: McGraw-Hill, 1976.

Lee, E. C., and Bowen, F. M. *Managing Multicampus Systems: Effective Administration in an Unsteady State.* San Francisco: Jossey-Bass, 1975.

Leslie, L. "The Financial Prospects for Higher Education in the 1980s." Unpublished paper, Center for the Study of Higher Education, University of Arizona, April 20, 1979.

Levine, C. H. "Organizational Decline and Cutback Management." *Public Administration Review,* 1978, *38*(4), 316-325.

Liaison Committee of the State Board of Education and the Regents of the University of California. *A Master Plan for Higher Education in California, 1960-1975.* Sacramento: California State Department of Education, 1960.

Lindblom, C. E. *The Policy Making Process.* Englewood Cliffs, N.J.: Prentice-Hall, 1968.

McCorkle, C. O., Jr. "Information for Institutional Decision Making." In C. R. Adams (Ed.), *New Directions for Institutional Research: Appraising Information Needs of Decision Makers,* no. 15. San Francisco: Jossey-Bass, 1977.

McGuire, J. W. (Ed.). *Contemporary Management: Issues and Viewpoints.* Englewood Cliffs, N.J.: Prentice-Hall, 1974.

Machiavelli, N. *The Prince and the Discourses.* (Translated by L. Ricci; revised by E. R. P. Vincent.) New York: Modern Library, 1950. (Originally published, 1513.)

Massy, W. F. "A Dynamic Equilibrium Model for University Budget Planning." *Management Science,* 1976, *23*(3), 248-256.

Mayhew, L. B. *Surviving the Eighties: Strategies and Procedures for Solving Fiscal and Enrollment Problems.* San Francisco: Jossey-Bass, 1979.

Merewitz, L., and Sosnick, S. H. *The Budget's New Clothes.* Chicago: Rand McNally, 1971.

Miles, R. E., and Snow, C. C. *Organizational Strategy, Structure, and Process.* New York: McGraw-Hill, 1978.

Millett, J. D. *The Academic Community.* New York: McGraw-Hill, 1962.

Millett, J. D. *Planning in Higher Education.* Washington, D.C.: Academy of Educational Development, 1977.

Millett, J. D. *New Structures of Campus Power: Success and Failures of Emerging Forms of Institutional Governance.* San Francisco: Jossey-Bass, 1978.

Millett, J. D. *Management, Governance, and Leadership.* New York: AMACOM, 1980.

Mondy, R., Holmes, R. E., and Flippo, E. B. *Management: Concepts and Practices.* Boston: Allyn & Bacon, 1980.

Mortimer, K. P., and McConnell, T. R. *Sharing Authority Effectively: Participation, Interaction, and Discretion.* San Francisco: Jossey-Bass, 1978.

Munitz, B. "Examining Administrative Performance." In P. Jedamus, M. W. Peterson, and Associates, *Improving Academic Management: A Handbook of Planning and Institutional Research.* San Francisco: Jossey-Bass, 1980.

Murdick, R. G. "MIS for MBO." *Journal of Systems Management,* March 1977, pp. 34-40.

National Association of College and University Business Officers. *Annual Survey of Endowment Funds of 144 Colleges and Universities.* Washington, D.C.: National Association of College and University Business Officers, 1978.

National Center for Education Statistics, U.S. Department of Health, Education and Welfare. *Digest of Educational Statistics.* Annual. Washington, D.C.: U.S. Government Printing Office, 1978, 1979, 1980.

O'Neill, J. *Resource Use in Higher Education: Trends in Outputs and Inputs, 1930-1967.* Berkeley, Calif.: Carnegie Commission on Higher Education, 1971.

Odiorne, G. S. *Management by Objectives.* New York: Pitman, 1965.

Odiorne, G. S. *The Change Resisters.* Englewood Cliffs, N.J.: Prentice-Hall, 1981.

Orwig, M. D., and Caruthers, J. K. "Selecting Budget Strategies and Priorities." In P. Jedamus, M. W. Peterson, and Associates, *Improving Academic Management: A Handbook of Planning and Institutional Research.* San Francisco: Jossey-Bass, 1980.

Pace, C. R. *Measuring Outcomes of College: Fifty Years of Findings and Recommendations for the Future.* San Francisco: Jossey-Bass, 1979.

Peterson, M. W. "Analyzing Alternative Approaches to Planning." In P. Jedamus, M. W. Peterson, and Associates, *Improving Academic Management: A Handbook of Planning and Institutional Research.* San Francisco: Jossey-Bass, 1980.

Phyrr, P. A. *Zero-Base Budgeting: A Practical Management Tool for Evaluating Expenses.* New York: Wiley, 1973.

Pusey, N. M. *American Higher Education 1945-1970: A Personal Report.* Cambridge, Mass.: Harvard University Press, 1978.

Quinn, J. B. *Strategies for Change: Logical Incrementalism.* Homewood, Ill.: Irwin, 1980.

Richman, B. M., and Farmer, R. N. *Leadership, Goals, and Power in Higher Education: A Contingency and Open-Systems Approach to Effective Management.* San Francisco: Jossey-Bass, 1974.

Schroeder, R. G. "Resource Planning in University Management by Goal-Programming." *Operations Research,* 1974, *22,* 700-710.

Smith, D. D. "Multi-Campus System Approaches to Academic Program Evaluation." In E. C. Craven (Ed.), *New Directions for Institutional Research: Alternative Models of Academic Program Evaluation,* no. 27. San Francisco: Jossey-Bass, 1980.

Steiner, G. A. *Top Management Planning.* New York: Macmillan, 1969.

Turksen, I. B., and Holzman, A. G. "Short Range Planning for Educational Management." Paper presented at 38th meeting of Operations Research Society of America, October 1970.

Uhl, N. *Encouraging Convergence of Opinion Through the Use of the Delphi Technique in the Process of Identifying an Institution's Goals.* Princeton, N.J.: Educational Testing Service, 1971.

U.S. Bureau of the Census. *Characteristics of Students.* Washington, D.C.: U.S. Bureau of the Census, 1976.

U.S. National Science Foundation. *Expenditures for Scientific Research at Universities and Colleges.* Annual. Washington, D.C.: U.S. National Science Foundation, 1979a, 1980.

U.S. National Science Foundation. *Federal Funds for Research and Development.* Annual. Washington, D.C.: U.S. National Science Foundation, 1979b.

U.S. Office of Education, Bureau of Student Financial Assistance. *Program Book.* Washington, D.C.: U.S. Office of Education, 1979.

University of California. *Academic Plan Phase II: The University-wide Perspective.* Vol. 1. Berkeley: Systemwide Administration, University of California, 1975a.

University of California. *Academic Plan Phase II: The Chancellors' Statements.* Vol. 2. Berkeley: Systemwide Administration, University of California, 1975b.

University of California. *Administrative Information in the University of California: The Report of a Task Force.* Berkeley: Systemwide Administration, University of California, 1976.

University of California. *Systemwide Administration.* Berkeley: Systemwide Administration, University of California, 1977a.

University of California. *The University of California Libraries: A Plan for Development.* Berkeley: Systemwide Administration, University of California, 1977b.

University of California. *Handbook of Program Review.* Berkeley: Systemwide Administration, University of California, 1978.

University of Wisconsin. *Summary of University of Wisconsin System Academic Program Audit and Review.* Academic Information Series No. 4. Madison: Office of Academic Affairs, University of Wisconsin System, 1977.

Walker, D. E. *The Effective Administrator: A Practical Approach to Problem Solving, Decision Making, and Campus Leadership.* San Francisco: Jossey-Bass, 1979.

Wallhaus, R. A. "Analyzing Academic Program Resource Requirements." In P. Jedamus, M. W. Peterson, and Associates,

Improving Academic Management: A Handbook of Planning and Institutional Research. San Francisco: Jossey-Bass, 1980.

Weathersby, G. B., and Balderston, F. E. "PPBS in Higher Education Planning and Management." *Higher Education,* 1972, *2,* 191-205.

Western Interstate Commission for Higher Education, National Institute of Independent Colleges and Universities, and Teachers Insurance and Annuity Association. *High School Graduates: Projections for the Fifty States.* Boulder, Colo.: Western Interstate Commission for Higher Education, 1979.

Wildavsky, A. "The Self-Evaluating Organization." *Public Administration Review,* 1972, *32*(5), 509-520.

✌✌✌ Index